Steve Hemphill has ⋯
about heaven that is t⋯
very imaginative and entertaining. You will enjoy every
word as the book builds your hope for the LORD's return
and your expectation of the blessings of eternity.

—Dr. David R. Reagan

Founder and director, Lamb & Lion Ministries

I am jealous of Steve. What a gift to have a great dad.
Dads, this is a must read so you can learn from one who
did it up right.

—Dr. Donald E. Anderson

President, Bible Teaching Resources

In My Search for the Real Heaven, Steve Hemphill
takes us on an exploration of Scripture and the imagination that allows us to leap forward in our journey home.
For those of us who have lost loved ones, the material
presented here makes the prospect of arriving at the
heavenly reunion sweeter than ever.

—Dr. Bill Richardson

Director, Center for Advanced Ministry Training,

Harding University.

my search *for the*
Real Heaven

Steve Hemphill

my search *for the*
Real Heaven

TATE PUBLISHING *& Enterprises*

Published by Tate Publishing & Enterprises, LLC
127 E. Trade Center Terrace | Mustang, Oklahoma 73064 USA
1.888.361.9473 | www.tatepublishing.com

Tate Publishing is committed to excellence in the publishing industry. The company reflects the philosophy established by the founders, based on Psalm 68:11,
"The LORD *gave the word and great was the company of those who published it."*

Book design copyright © 2009 by Tate Publishing, LLC. All rights reserved.
Cover design by Lance Waldrop
Interior design by Jeff Fisher

Published in the United States of America

ISBN: 978-1-60799-023-9
1. Religion, Christian Life, Death, Grief, Bereavement
2. Religion, Christianity, United Church of Christ, Congregational
09.05.08

Dedication

Stay with it to the end. You won't be sorry, and you'll be saved. All during this time, the good news—the Message of the kingdom—will be preached all over the world, a witness staked out in every country. And then the end will come.

Matthew 24:13-14 (The Message)

My Search for the Real Heaven is dedicated to my dad, Jamie Voigt Hemphill, who was an inspiration to his family and to countless others. He wore many titles: dad, counselor, friend, coach, minister, rock mason, farmer, carpenter, teacher, church elder, leader, encourager, cousin, uncle, friend, and to his six grandsons, Peepaw. He gave of himself, and his time to do everything he could to encourage others and help enlarge the kingdom of God. He was loved by all, and he loved all. I once heard it said of Will Rogers that he never met a man he didn't like. That describes Dad.

After his untimely death in the summer of 2000, many people told our family of ways Dad had encouraged them in one form or another. His funeral was so packed with people that every seat in the auditorium was full. The aisles were crowded with people who were willing to stand throughout the service, the fellowship hall was full (these people could hear the service but were unable to see any of it), and some had to park blocks away and walk in the sweltering heat of that hot August day. I even talked to friends who had driven an hour to attend, and after seeing the crowd standing outside the building trying to get in, resigned themselves to drive home without even getting out of their cars.

That's the kind of man he was. Is. Will be forever. He has gone on to his reward, unspeakable joy in the presence of his Savior and his fellow believers.

I miss him. I will continue to do so until our reunion. This is why I dedicate this book in his memory. But he would also want honor to be given to every godly father. Godly fathers are rare in Scripture and rare today as well. So I dedicate this book to all godly fathers in an effort to give honor where honor is due. My life has been less difficult because of a godly father, and I hope that the inspiration from this story of my godly father will cause many others to follow that pathway.

In his honor, a tithe of the proceeds from this book will be given in his name to the Seth Rogers Retreat Center and Camp Deer Run in Winnsboro, Texas. This organization helps more young people to begin their kingdom walk than any other I know of.

Another tithe will be given to one of the most important efforts on the planet: to send the gospel message of Jesus Christ through Faith Comes By Hearing.

Faith Comes by Hearing (faithcomesbyhearing.com) began in the 1970s with Bible audiocassettes. People would purchase these cassettes and send them to their missionaries around the world. The missionaries would say, "This is great, but I need it in Spanish, German, or French." So they began to do that.

As of this writing, the organization now has the New Testament Audio Bibles available in 359 languages and have ingeniously put it on a memory chip inside the Proclaimer. The Proclaimer is a self-contained unit with a solar recharge panel and a speaker that enables a large audience to hear God's Word in group listening sessions. Since over half the world's population is illiterate, I believe this is the best possible way to get the Good News about Jesus out to a lost and dying world.

So be warmed and encouraged that your purchase of this work is attempting to glorify God by (a) encouraging everyone to focus on and get excited about our eternal existence and (b) helping to get the Bible out in a format that will reach more people than ever before. Thank you, and may God bless you with a deeper and better understanding of the eternal riches and joys in store for you.

Dear LORD, *I pray that the words I have to say will inspire all who read to realize their need.*

I hope that everything I wrote opens up countless eyes, causing many to be wise.

I plead mankind will be freed to serve you in deeds working to meet the needs of lost souls.

LORD, *my King, I long to wear your ring, showing I belong to your happy throng of saved people.*

I pray that until the day you return for me, I will be pleasing you as I long to do, day and night,

helping make things right. In Jesus' name, Amen.

Your servant, Steve Hemphill

Table of Contents

Foreword

I believe that we are living in historic times. The stock market dropped (again), real-estate is bust, and the automobile industry is looking poorly. Promised bipartisan politics are a thing of the past. The old moral majority seems to be shrinking to a minority, and Christian persecution is escalating around the globe. When I survey the condition of the world at hand, I get a sinking feeling.

However, there is a light at the end of the tunnel, and it's not an oncoming locomotive. It's the light of hope, and Steve Hemphill has captured the essence of that light in *My Search for the Real Heaven*. While our generation seems suspended in that ever-darkening tunnel of bad news and difficulties, Steve gently nudges us forward with fresh perspective: we are beings built for eternity; built for the Light.

Steve invites his readers on a time-travel journey through a *chat-over-a-glass-of-ice-tea writing style*. Looking back to the past, he shares intimate details of his life with an ideal father— the father we all long for and will experience in Christ. Then Steve fast forwards readers into the future where we get an inside look at his earthly father's arrival in heaven. It's the stuff dreams are made of, and it's all biblical.

For anyone who's curious about the hereafter or unsure of God's eternal plan, this is a must read. For those who've lost confidence in humanity, this book serves as a reminder that when Christ lives in us, we can be a bright light on a dark planet.

Passion for heaven is evident in both this book and in Steve's actions. He's donating proceeds to a ministry I am a part of: *Faith Come By Hearing*. Because Steve wants people from every tribe, nation, and tongue to know the truth about eternity, he's seeing to it that those without access to God's Word receive it and receive it in a language and format that they can understand.

Steve Hemphill is cheering us all to heaven. We'd be wise to turn the page and head that way.

—Laurie Westlake

Faith Comes By Hearing

The Story Begins

Everybody who lived in Lydda and Sharon saw him walking around and woke up to the fact that God was alive and active among them.

Acts 9:35 (The Message)

Background

About a year ago, a friend called one morning and almost frantically said, "I have to eat lunch with you today." I agreed. At lunch he was fidgety and nervous. I asked what was wrong, and he cautiously replied, "I'm supposed to tell you something, and I'm nervous. God wants you to write about your dad."

Dad had been dead almost four years when this occurred, but Dad's death was still too fresh in my mind for me to put any thoughts or memories down on paper. I tried to write, but the words just didn't flow out right. So I sort of forgot about the whole thing. I had given it the old college try, hadn't I?

Almost a year later, there was a large article on the front page of the religious section of the local paper. The story was about a Christian writer's conference coming up at a nearby Christian school. I threw it away after having only read the headline. I had no goal to become a writer. But the story wouldn't go away. Not for me. A close friend saw the same story. He came by my office and laid a fifty-dollar bill on my desk and said, "Here, I'm paying your entry fee for that Christian writer's conference. Will you go?"

I said I needed to check our family calendar and indicated that I would go if we had no conflicts on that date. I hoped there was a conflict, but I felt quite safe with that answer, since our busy schedule with work, church, and three teenage boys rarely allows for a free Saturday. He accepted that answer but followed up with me the next day, reminding me of the promise I had made to go if I had no conflict. Reluctantly, I had to relent and register, since it just happened to be one of those rare Saturdays when we were completely free. I went.

I have rarely felt so out of place. Most of the attendees had set the lofty goal of becoming a published author. I had no such goal. In fact, I didn't even want to be there. But I felt obligated to stay until early afternoon, and enjoy the free lunch provided, since free is in my price range. The morning sessions were interesting, but about as riveting as watching a cork bobber at the end of a fishing line on a pond with no fish. Lunch was nothing to write home about, but it was free. But after lunch, an earthquake shook my world. This quake was to have repercussions for months and probably years to come. It ended up shaking my soul to the core in ways that I was incapable of understanding. Scary ways. Overwhelming ways. Emotional ways. The earthquake had a name. Faye Field.

I should have known something was up when the room scheduled for her presentation filled up to overflowing. Maybe I should have left. If I'd known what I was in for, I would have. But I didn't. They ran out of chairs, so I sat there on the floor in total shock. I felt like a panicked deer caught in the headlights of an oncoming car. He can't move quickly enough. He just stands there. That's what I did too. I stayed. The title of her presentation was "Inspirational Writing." Little did I know how inspirational she would be.

When we moved to a much larger room, I think I knew deep down that I was in trouble. It's not that I was conscious of the danger; I just sort of instinctively got as far away from Mrs. Field as I could. I went to the back row on the far side of the room from where she sat. I felt safer there. I wasn't. Far from it. I was about as safe as that deer when the impact is one second away.

Mrs. Field was a local. She sat in a comfortable chair, smiling sweetly, and eyed us like a cat that notices someone left the birdcage open, and the bird doesn't know it yet. She would sit in that chair throughout her talk. Now I call it the chair of power. That little ninety-three-year-old lady was one of the most inspirational speakers I've ever heard. Once the introduction was over and they turned her loose to speak. The energy and enthusiasm in her voice would make you think she was twenty-three. She had the audience in a trance. Although the room was packed full of people, there was complete silence as she spoke about her life. The only noise I noticed other than her sweet-sounding voice during the next hour was the laughter that exploded regularly as she relayed the amazing story of her life as an inspirational writer. If I live to be ninety-three myself, a scary thought, I will never forget her speech.

Any description I would write wouldn't do her justice. But I can tell you that the people in that room were hanging on her every word. I've been to Promise Keepers; I've been to gatherings all over the country; I've heard motivational speakers, preachers, and professional presenters regularly during my fifty-plus years on this planet, but I've never heard anything like Faye Field.

She started and ended with a prayer. She talked about home. She talked about God and heaven. She made our hearts come alive as we journeyed with her through a life of ups and downs. She kept saying, "Write what's in your heart. God put it there. Don't worry about trying to write what the editors want. My husband always said that the editors don't know what they want half the time, anyway. If God wants you to write, he will open the door to being published. Just trust him. And remember, the pen is mightier than the sword. You can change the world with your writing. Now go out there and change it!"

I felt just like I did when my old football coach got us ready for that all-important district game with our archrivals, Sonora. When Coach Burns finished his pre-game speech, we were sure we could have beaten the Dallas Cowboys in Texas Stadium.

Although I really knew that wasn't true, after hearing Mrs. Field, we all felt like we could actually change the world.

I went home from the conference without a clue as to how my world was about to change. When I got to work on Monday morning, I discovered my hard drive had crashed, and we were going to have to replace it and then restore all the programs and data. A major undertaking, as you can imagine. So while my computer tech was doing all that, I was twiddling my thumbs. I decided to get my laptop out of my truck and take a crack at inspirational writing. I had been doing some studying lately on heaven, so I decided to talk about a few of the amazing glimpses we see in Scripture about heaven. I typed the title. But something happened when I started typing—something strange and emotional.

I intended to write a sentence or two of introduction before getting into a study of the verses, but it didn't stop there. In fact, it didn't stop for almost a thousand words. It's one of the weirdest things that's ever happened to me. The brief introduction led to a quick overview of my childhood. All these sentences and paragraphs came spilling out. It went everywhere. It went all over me and all over the floor. I couldn't stop it, not even if I wanted to. And I was in too much shock to know if I wanted to. It almost felt embarrassing, as if I'd spilled catsup on my shirt with everyone looking.

Tears flowed freely as the words spilled onto my laptop and the white page just in front of the blinking curser. At least, I think that's what happened, since my eyes were so blurry. I couldn't stop it. It came in surges that overwhelmed and weakened me with each wave. As each paragraph spilled out of me, I grabbed a quick breath and changed the subject in a feeble attempt to turn it off. But I couldn't. When it was over, I could barely function. As I re-lived these childhood experiences in my mind, I realized what a special home and family I have had. Those bottled-up words were bound to spill out sooner or later, but I didn't realize it until this first bloodletting of words was over.

When the overwhelming emotions finally began to subside, I knew what I had to do. I had to call my friend who told me that God wanted me to write about Dad. He said, "I'll be there in thirty minutes."

I told him about the experience, and I handed him the pages to read for himself. Initially, I was relieved. *Great,* I thought, *I got that out of my system and now I can move on. When he finishes reading, that chapter of my life will be over.* Nothing could have been further from the truth.

As he read the story, his eyes were red with emotion too. But when he finished, he said the five most dreaded words I think I ever heard, "Where's the rest of it?"

"What do you mean the 'rest' of it? That's it!"

"No, it isn't. It may take you years, but you have to finish it. God wants you to finish it. You have no choice."

I laid my head on the table and cried. I didn't want to.

"God will give you strength," he said.

I pray that the words in this story about my father will inspire you to meditate on your eternal home just as much as Mrs. Field's words have inspired me to write them. With that backdrop, let me open the curtain on my life and let you have a peek into my world. Enjoy.

Memories of Home

Do you ever think about heaven? Do you ever try to imagine what it will be like? I do. All the time since my dad died. I scoured the Scriptures looking for all the "glimpses of heaven" I could find.

I miss him. Dad was a friendly, humble, serving gentleman, the kind of man who's getting harder and harder to find. He was the mayor of my hometown when he died, a small town of about two thousand. Mason, Texas, was a place anyone would be proud to be from. We lived a block from the downtown square, and I walked there often as a little boy. Big, tall pecan trees filled our front yard on a street called "Live Oak." What a place to grow up. My brother and I played daily in that yard, often climbing the trees and pretending we were on a far-off adventure. The memories flood my heart even now as I remember that special time and place, a world where everything was right with God. It was fireflies in the back yard just after the sun sank low. It was the smell of homemade cookies that had just come out of the oven. It was that special scent of something fried—anything fried. It was a red ant bed cropping up by the back door. It was the neighbor yelling, "Hello, boys" as they pulled into the carport across the street. It was the sound of the sheep in the fenced vacant lot behind the house. It was building a secret fort in the scrub brush down the hill out of cardboard boxes from Underwood's Food Store. It was Mama yelling into the woods, "Supper's ready!" And it was the excitement when we heard those truly magic words: "Daddy's home!"

Daddy is home. Now he's gone, and he really is home. I miss him.

He had been the announcer at the football stadium for the home games for thirty-eight years. He had a strong, soothing voice as he called out the results of each play and told us who got the tackle or caught the pass. He sang the national anthem solo on the microphone every week. People still come up to Mom to tell her they miss that. So do I.

He became sort of an icon in that little town. It was special to him. It meant something to live in a place like that. He served the community without the thought of *what's in it for me?*

What really made him special was his propensity to help people. I saw it over and over during my formative years. We might be very involved in a family project or some repair job on the house, but if someone came by asking for help or advice, we dropped what we were doing and went immediately to see what we could do to help. It never ceased to amaze me. The pattern never changed—he did it again and again.

Often, someone needed advice. A friend might show up in his cowboy hat and pointy-toed boots—the kind you can use to kill a roach in the corner—and say to dad, "Jamie, I need to talk to you 'bout somethin.'" Sometimes we were given hasty instructions on how to continue the project without Dad's oversight, and sometimes he said, "Boys, go play a few minutes while I talk to Mr. Reeves." We were thrilled at the chance for a break. The hot sun on the central Texas landscape was always a nuisance. We might head out to the cardboard fort or hit the swings or—and this was really fun—we would climb the antenna pole by the corner of the back porch to play on the roof.

It sounds funny to even say that now, but we actually did play on the roof. Mom couldn't keep us off the roof. What a great view we had from up there. We could see the top of the old rock courthouse in the center of the square from the highest peak on that roof. We could see the hill where Fort Mason once stood. We could look eye-to-eye with the birds in their nests near the top of those pecan trees. We felt like we were on top of the world. Sometimes I wish I could still get that feeling. We would look down at Dad whispering attentively in the dirt driveway to whoever needed advice for the day from the man we called "Dad."

What a man. What a heart. How kind he was. How serving. What an example.

But now he's gone. He's gone home, his *real* home, his heavenly home. Someday I'll join him. The family reunion under the shade of those big pecan trees will include cloth-covered tables straining under a feast of pie, fried chicken, and homemade rolls that will make our mouths water. What a great time we'll have.

But that's for later. Right now, I have my own responsibilities. My own boys need my attention, my example, my time, my love. The reunion with Dad will have to wait. But I look forward to that time with great anticipation. "Love ya, Dad, miss ya, Dad," I often say to his picture by my bed. "Thanks for the memories and for the Christian example you always were. See ya soon!"

What Might Be: Arrival

"Hello, Jamie. It's time for your transfer to the real world. It's time to go home. I'm your escort. Here, let me carry you.

"I know you have a lot of questions, so let me explain a few things. I have been assigned to you for all of your sixty-nine-year stay on Earth. Other angels have helped at critical moments, and some were assigned to your family—your wife Mary, and your sons Steve and Kendal—but I have been with you all along. Just as it says in Hebrews 1:14, 'Angels are only servants. They are spirits sent from God to care for those who will receive salvation.' I am simply one of his servants.

"Now that your time has come, I will escort you to the safety and beauty of intermediate heaven, where you will enjoy paradise in fellowship with the Savior, the saints, and your relatives and friends who have preceded you in death. We call this intermediate heaven, because your final home is still under construction. It is being built from the good deeds you did for the kingdom that are the building blocks of your permanent home, and more raw materials are being sent up every day by those you influenced for the kingdom. In other words, your good deeds that caused others to do good deeds are added to your account. In the end, you will have quite a home here, because the Audience of One is well aware of all your unselfish acts of kindness to others. You have put his kingdom first for most of your earthly life. For this reason, the final judgment where all your rewards will be presented must wait. This also allows your descendants to enjoy your reward ceremony.

"You are about to take your first breath of heaven's air. You will likely cough and gag as you did when you took your first earthly breath, but not for the same reason. The atmosphere of the shadow land (earth) is rank with the smell of sulfur, caused by sin, and the shame of mankind's fall. It is so full of ugliness caused by the curse of sin that we are amazed you can breathe at all. When you cough and gag on your first heavenly breath, it is to remove the last of the stench caused by the environment of fallen earth. After that, you will scarcely be able to believe how pure and wonderful the air of heaven smells. Fill your lungs with it. Enjoy it to the fullest. You never have to breathe the stench again.

"I'm taking you to the real world. The world you were made for. And you will be with the One who made it all just for you. He loves you more than you can possibly know. All angels have trouble understanding the King's plan to save mankind, but we know that you—not we—were created to be his image-bearers. We are his servants, sent to serve those who will be saved. I am honored to have been with you.

"When I deliver you safely, I must be on my way to my next assignment. My next task is on the opposite side of the world, and I am needed there very soon. We will meet again.

"Your first pleasure in the new world will be a welcome party. Many old acquaintances will be renewed, and many you have never met are eager to greet you. I will see you again soon."

With that, the escorting angel left in a flash of light. Then the party welcome party began.

aug 17 work 12 - 1:30
steady steps

at home (get eggs at
9¢ lettuce church)

papers on table
income tax

store
whipping cream
bananas

Barbara's
internet
put picture on singles?
or send email's?

rake yard

work 18th 8 to 1:30
steady
steps

Introduction

"I heard a voice thunder from the Throne: 'Look! Look! God has moved into the neighborhood, making his home with men and women'!"

Revelation 21:3 (The Message)

Home for the Weekend

After I graduated from Mason High School in 1975 and left home for college at Abilene Christian University, home was never the same. It was a whole new world for me. New friends. Exciting experiences. Fresh opportunities. Sure, I went home for the weekend for a quick visit, often just to get Mom to wash my clothes and taste some home cooking. But I was so excited about the future, a future away from the small hick town I grew up in, that I didn't really appreciate what I had. Isn't that true of us all? We don't know what we have until it's gone.

Now it's different. I'm over fifty, complete with all the aches and pains that come with that privilege, and "home for the weekend" has a completely different feeling. Now home for the weekend means arriving late on Friday night and unloading all our gear in the dark with a flashlight. It means talking until late at night by lamplight or sitting in the old swing in the yard. It's the smell of fresh sugar cookies or pie crust. I love pie crust. When I was a little kid, mom always took the scrap pieces of pie crust that were left over from baking a pecan pie and lay them out flat on an old cookie sheet. She carefully spread butter all over, nice and even. Then she sprinkled a liberal portion of sugar and cinnamon and baked it in the oven. Man, you talk about something good! It's the feel of the air that surrounds and permeates every square inch of that town, a town I no longer call hick. It's a special place; it's home.

Home for the weekend makes you feel relaxed, special, wanted, loved. Don't you wish you could stay in that place? Don't you wish you could feel that way all the time? Don't you know that if you could bottle and sell that "home for the weekend" feeling you'd be rich?

Some day, that feeling will be permanent. We'll stay in that place of comfort because we will be home. You've got a Friend, someone who gave up his heavenly home and went off to Earth University for your sake. He's gone back home, and he's adding on to his Father's house to make room for you. You're so special to him that he's building that room to the exact specifications he knows you'll like.

Your eternal clothing is also special. It's provided by—you! According to Revelation 19:7-8, the good deeds you do for his kingdom are your eternal clothing for home, your real home, your permanent home, your heavenly home. Now let's begin our study about it! Hold on, it's going to be an exciting ride!

An Unattractive Heaven

I have found that when many Christians are asked what we'll do in heaven, we either stare back with blank faces or describe how we will be floating spirits on clouds playing the harp and worshiping God all day every day. This view doesn't even get *Christians* excited about eternity in heaven, much less the world. Too often, we have formed our opinion of heaven by what our parents or church leaders think rather than an honest, open evaluation of the Scriptures themselves.

I honestly believe that an inaccurate, unattractive view of our eternal future actually works to hinder our attitude toward evangelism. Why try to convert someone else to an eternal future that we aren't even excited about? You may not agree with every idea suggested here as we evaluate the Bible verses together about heaven, but I hope you will listen, meditate, and pray for insight, because if I'm right, heaven is a place to really get excited about! Ultimately, my goal is to get you so excited about heaven that you can't stand to be silent about it! I hope you can appreciate that goal in spite of a disagreement about an idea presented. But remember, this is not a salvation issue, and it's all right if we don't all agree on every point presented.

The Christian Goal

How do Olympic athletes endure the hardship and discipline of all the years of training and preparation? By picturing themselves on the podium receiving the gold medal and hearing their national anthem in the presence of a cheering crowd. What is the goal of Christians? Heaven. Do we think or study much about it? No.

Biblical Deductive Reasoning

In the evaluation of any biblical subject, we must often read between the lines or learn to use what I call, "biblical deductive reasoning." Let me explain what I mean with an example.

Where do kangaroos live? Kangaroos live in Australia. Other than zoos, are kangaroos indigenous to any other areas on earth? No. Have kangaroos ever lived in the Middle East? Of course not! Are you sure?

Where did the ark land after the flood? Mount Ararat. Where is Mount Ararat? It's in the Middle East. Now, let me repeat the question: have kangaroos ever lived in the Middle East? Yes!

You were required to use biblical deductive reasoning and common sense to come to a conclusion that now contradicts your original position! Are you damaged in any way from changing your stance? No. Are you more enlightened instead? Maybe. I hope so.

That's what I hope and pray happens to you as you consider the ideas in this book.

Scriptural Authority

God invented everything. This includes language and our ability to communicate. Out of all the possible ways he could have led us to truth and salvation, he chose words. Isn't it probably safe to say that he made sure he used the right ones?

> God's Law is more real and lasting than the stars in the sky and the ground at your feet. Long after stars burn out and earth wears out, God's Law will be alive and working. Trivialize even the smallest item in God's Law, and you will only have trivialized yourself. But take it seriously, show the way for others, and you will find honor in the kingdom.
>
> Matthew 5:18-19 (The Message)

> All Scripture is God-breathed and is useful for teaching, rebuking, correcting and training in righteousness, so that the man of God may be thoroughly equipped for every good work.
>
> 2 Timothy 3:16-17 (NIV)

So if you desire to know more about heaven, where do you go to make sure you get the truth? All Scripture.

Note also that the Holy Spirit is involved and active in your personal discovery of truth, including the truth about heaven: "When the Spirit of truth comes, he will guide you into all truth. He will not speak on his own but will tell you what he has heard. He will tell you about the future" (John 16:13, NLT).

I have been diligently studying passages on heaven since my dad left for that destination in August of 2000. I have come to the conclusion that it takes prayer, desire, wisdom, and biblical deductive reasoning to get a glimpse of heaven to embed in our heart. So let's start with a prayer.

Beginning Prayer

LORD, *I pray that every single person who reads this book or hears the summary of its ideas are blessed with enlightenment, encouragement, and renewed in their zeal to live in heaven when they die. And as we embark on this study about our eternal home, open our eyes, ears, hearts, and minds to the truth about our future with you. Don't let Satan deceive us into believing heaven will be dull or boring in any way. Please reveal kingdom secrets to us as we study and give us insight and wisdom to properly understand. In Jesus's name, Amen.*

What Might Be: The Five Earths of Scripture

"Hello, Jamie, I'm a servant of the King, sent to instruct you on some of the major events of the earths of the histories."

"The histories? What are the histories?"

"The histories are what we call the record books that document all things done by the King from creation until new earth."

"New earth? What's new earth?"

"It never ceases to amaze us how even those like you who have extensive biblical knowledge must be taught and trained on some of the most basic realities of Scripture. New earth is part of your eternal future.

"The Bible clearly discusses five unique earths. The first earth is original creation, sinless and perfect. In fact, what many believers fail to realize is that original earth was part of heaven, part of the home of God. You could picture it as his garden, the garden of God, Eden.

"Original earth was perfect in every way. It was similar to a crib for a baby that you would provide for your own. There were no thorns, no stickers, no poison, no pains or diseases of any kind, and especially no death. This is why the King could walk freely, daily with Adam. A pure and holy God could not tolerate contact with a place of disease or death without the purification fires to insulate him. Sinai was a perfect example: when he later descended onto Sinai, the earth was under the curse, so flames like those from a furnace prevented actual contact. Not so in the garden. He walked daily with all of creation because everything was good.

"After sin temporarily separated the King from physical contact with creation, the borders of heaven were redrawn, so to speak; original earth was expelled from direct contact with the Holy. This was necessary for your own safety. The purification fires would have annihilated all life. However, those fires discussed throughout the Bible and particularly in Peter's letters will one day cleanse and purify earth in preparation for the fourth earth of Scripture, restored earth. But I'm getting ahead of myself. I'll come back to that.

"So the first earth of the Bible was the original, good, perfect, pure earth. The second earth was the cursed earth.

"How sad we all were to see the deterioration, and how different every part of creation became when the King placed a curse on the perfect world that brought so much trouble and misery. All of a sudden, to our dismay, roses had sharp thorns, the rainforests of what would later become North Africa became a desert eventually called Sahara. Stickers appeared, making the beautiful became ugly. Colors faded worldwide, their brightness gone. Strong, lovely smells that had once permeated flowers, grasses, and trees became a mere shadow of what they were before.

"Adam and Eve began to defecate, urinate, cry, experience pain, get sick, and, worst of all, die. We wailed in pain with them, although unseen. We watched in sorrow and sadness as the world deteriorated from a pristine beauty to a smelly, ugly, complete mess in comparison. In fact, words cannot describe the loss or the remorse that filled both Creator and creation at the time.

"Adam and Eve were never the same. Unhappiness now dominated their emotions, and, although they experienced the joy of family and children over the next nine hundred years or so, they also saw that the children would die too.

"The first blood was shed when the King killed some innocent lambs and gave mankind their first clothes. These died to cover sin. According to the King, it was the only way. Death and blood were the requirements for life to continue. We all hoped it would end there, but it was not to be. Soon Cain killed Abel, and this first murder led to countless others. We felt the misery and cried with the King. It looked like it wouldn't stop, like mankind would wipe himself out as they fought over women, gold, and positions of authority, but God had a plan.

"We were all so shocked with the mayhem and madness planet-wide that we missed what the King saw: one family godly enough to save and start over! I admit, we were all confused when we heard God say he was going to destroy the earth. We thought destruction meant annihilation! Not to God. He told Noah to build a boat so they could be rescued from the destruction. Over the centuries, we have come to understand that when God brings judgment, the good are saved by the same mechanism that the evil is purged. In this case, the flood wiped out and destroyed all the evil people but saved the good ones.

"This brings us to the third earth in Scripture: the postflood earth. And again, although it was much diminished from the original and even from the cursed earth, it was habitable. And, to eyes that had never seen the previous version, even beautiful. Curious.

"Jamie, this was the planet you knew. You lived your life on the post-flood earth."

"Okay, I understand so far, but that's just three earths. You said there was five."

"Yes, there are five, but the last two are still to come, so we won't spend time going over them now, because you are able to see and experience them from your viewing port here! You will see with perfect clarity what the King will do with the improved vision you have as a Christian here in paradise!"

"Can't you tell me anything about them?"

"Well, I can lead you to a better understanding of them with the guidebook in your hand."

"Guidebook?"

"Forgive me, your Bible. What do you want to know?"

"Well, first of all, you speak of the first three earths as if they are separate ones. In reality, they're just three versions of the same one. How do you explain that?"

"I have no explanation, other than the fact that this is what the King calls them in his Holy Word."

"That's it? That's your explanation?"

"It's enough, because it's what the King provides. He always provides enough. His Word is Truth. Do you not agree?"

"Well, yes, of course, it's all just so new to me. And I thought that when I got to heaven, I would know everything!"

"You thought you would know everything? You thought you would be God? Only God knows everything; you have much to learn!"

"Yes, I apparently do. I just didn't know I would be learning in heaven."

"Don't be surprised. Heaven would be awfully dull and boring for you if you had nothing to learn, wouldn't it?"

Chapter 1: Literal Versus Symbolic

"It's really happened! The Master has been raised up—
Simon saw him!"

Luke 24:34 (The Message)

Dad's Special Sayings

When I was growing up, Dad often amused us—and himself—
with his special little funny sayings, little phrases he used for
things to throw us off guard or make us laugh. I sat down one
day to make a list of them. I remembered quite a few, but I'm
sure I couldn't remember them all. It was like being asked to tell
a joke. You feel put on the spot to think of one, so the pressure
to come up with one keeps you from being successful. But in the
daily flow of living and interacting, funny stories or jokes might
pop into your head and make you laugh right out loud. They
tickle your funny bone.

There were several periods when I was growing up that small
congregations within driving distance of our home were without a preacher. Sometimes Dad would agree to be their pulpit
minister for a few weeks, but it would end up being a lot longer.
He was fine with that. It might often take the congregation a
lot longer to find a full-time replacement than they expected,
so Dad would continue to preach, Sunday after Sunday, until a
final decision was made and the new man arrived to take over.

Melvin was one of those small towns where he preached for
an extended period of time. Melvin was a farming and ranch
community not too far from Brady, Texas. It took a little less
than an hour to get there from our house, and it was my favorite
place he ever preached.

What made it so special? I have to admit it was a little girl named Laurie. She was as cute as a bug. What made it even better was that her parents were usually the family who offered to have the preacher and his family—us—over for Sunday lunch. This meant I got to see Laurie all afternoon before Dad preached again Sunday evening. Then we'd drive home after Sunday night church.

Although I was only about nine or ten years old, I was in love. Laurie was beautiful. All girls were yucky before Laurie. She was perfect. I don't think I just sat there and stared, but it was all I could do to keep from it. She looked good. She smelled good. She smiled good. Her dad had land. It was perfect. Not only all that, but she liked to play hide-and-seek on the screened-in back porch at her house, just like I did! Could life get any better?

Another reason I liked going to their house for Sunday lunch was the meal itself. It was a real feast. I loved fried chicken, and her mama cooked a great fried chicken. Now what goes with fried chicken? The main side dish required was mashed potatoes and gravy. We always had mashed potatoes and gravy.

One Sunday, I was asked to pray before the meal. I was at that age when kids often pray for what they see on the table with one eye cracked open, "Thank you for the green beans, thank you for the fried chicken, thank you for the mashed potatoes, thank you for the gravy—oops, we haven't got any gravy!" I don't really remember it, but Mom said they laughed about it for years. Those were the days.

Anyway, the normal routine each Sunday was to rise early, drive to Melvin for Bible class and the morning service, go home with a member for lunch, enjoy the afternoon with that family, regroup for an evening service, and then drive back home to Mason that night. One particular Sunday night, I remember sitting in the front seat with Dad on the way home late that night when he said, "It sure is froggy tonight."

I looked out the window. "Where are the frogs?"

"I mean up in the air; it's hard to see the road very far ahead because it's so froggy," Dad laughingly replied. I laughed too because I realized it was another one of Dad's colloquialisms, and he had quite a few.

When I was leaving for college, he handed me a twenty-dollar bill. "Here, put this in the Hip National Bank." Dad called the billfold the Hip National. When we were tired of riding in the car on a long trip, he'd sometimes say, "Do y'all want a good laugh?" We screamed, "Yes!" thinking he had a good joke to tell us. He would respond with, "Okay, hold on just a minute. We'll pull over in just one mile and have a good laugh. There's a hysterical marker coming up." We kind of got tired of that one. But how I'd love to hear him say those words right now.

As we grew older we realized that Dad liked to kid around a lot, just to see us laugh and have a good time. He always wanted everyone around him to be having a good time. But Dad's light-hearted approach to daily life seemed to shift gears as he took on what he felt like was his most important role in life, teacher. When he put on his teacher hat, he got serious and everything came into clear focus. Why? Because God was focused, and his word—the Holy Bible—was sacred, worthy of honor and all our focused attention. You took it for what it said. You obeyed its instructions. You believed its stories. And unless the context made it clear that it wasn't, you took it literally. You couldn't always take Dad literally when he was fooling around, but he certainly took God's word literally.

The Father of Oceanography

Matthew Fontaine Maury was born on January 14, 1806. He is known worldwide as the father of oceanography. And he became that because he was an avid student of the Bible, and he believed in taking God's word literally.

He was studying his Bible one day and noticed a phrase in part of Psalm 8:

You made him ruler over the works of your hands; you

put everything under his feet: all flocks and herds, and the beasts of the field, the birds of the air, and the fish of the sea, all that swim the paths of the seas.

Psalm 8:6-8 (NIV)

Maury read this and said, "There are paths in the seas?" Then he set out to discover them. He did. He joined the U. S. Navy and was eventually promoted to the Superintendent of Charts. He required all Navy vessels to document their position along with water temperature and direction of the current. He collected and compiled this information until the water pathways of worldwide water currents were documented. This information led to the United States having a tremendous maritime advantage over all of their enemies. In 1855, he published *The Physical Geography of the Sea*, which is now known as the first textbook of modern oceanography. This all happened because he read the Bible and took it literally.

Are The Bible Stories True?

Is the Bible literal or just a collection of fictional stories designed to make us feel good? Some consider the Bible just symbolic stories about creation, a flood, and genealogies that lead to Jesus. Are the main events of the Bible meant to be taken as historical facts?

More and more, people of the world around us say that Jesus didn't really rise from the dead, it was probably a strong wind that parted the Red Sea, the pillar of fire by night and cloud by day that led Israel to Mt. Sinai and beyond was just a figment of their imagination, Goliath wasn't really nine feet tall, the fire from heaven that killed Nadab and Abihu was probably just lightning, and a talking snake in a place called Eden is just a fable.

The problem more and more is that, in general, Christians

have opened the door to this kind of thinking by agreeing to doubt whether Genesis 1 is literal or not.

"Jesus called over a child, whom he stood in the middle of the room, and said, 'I'm telling you, once and for all, that unless you return to square one and start over like children, you're not even going to get a look at the kingdom, let alone get in'" (Matthew 18:2-3, The Message).

Although we are taught by Jesus to have the faith of a child, if a child read Genesis 1, he or she would think that God made the world in six days. But, sadly, I have discovered that many Christians don't believe this anymore.

Newspaper Survey On The Afterlife

In an article by the Abilene Reporter News from September 30, 2007, writer Brian Bethel asked thirty-five different people this question: "What happens when you die?" The responses were interesting, and to a great degree, revealing. Here are a few excerpts from that article:

Benny Leija thinks that when we die, it's just like Rover—we're dead all over and that's it. He said, "When you die, [they] put you in the hole and that's it. Period…You're there, six to eight feet underground, little by little turning to dust."

Deborah Lorne thinks you need to become good enough to get to go to heaven. "Heaven must be earned."

Wendell Broom seems quite confused. "Time stops. All the body sensations cease. It is neither hot nor cold, light nor dark…You seem to be alone…no up or down, no gravity. No geography. No scenery. No seasons…no body… suspended in a conscious-but-directionless state."

Roy Newell also focuses on the intermediate time between death and the resurrection: "At the present time, all of God's chosen people are asleep in their graves, waiting for Christ to call them forth out of their graves to share in his eternal life for all eternity." He has completely forgotten Paul's opinion in 2

Corinthians 5:8 that to be absent from the body means that you are present with the LORD.

Martin Jones said we wouldn't have a body. "The life that we will experience after this life will be spiritual."

Frankie SoRelle thought we might or might not have a body. She said, "… we will be some spirit or body form like we are now."

Jennifer Rector states simply, "Heaven and hell are literal places."

Vanessa Lynn Chapman said, "… a place that has only been in my dreams. A place where I can hear the ocean waves crash against the sandy shoreline…where I can hear the wind rush through the enormous trees, making their leaves sing to me… Where I can see the brightest blue sky with giant, marshmallow puffy white clouds…where I can see the greenest, weed-free grass that I can sink my toes into and roll around in, laughing uncontrollably."

Paula Davis thinks the Scriptures mean it when they say our bodies will be transformed rather than eliminated or replaced. "We will receive bodies that are suitable for living for all of eternity in heaven."

Jim Needham believes that we will join other works for the King in this new environment. "We will participate with God in his endeavors."

Yvonne Carithers has thought about the scientific discoveries that reveal there are at least ten dimensions. We currently live in a four-dimensional world containing length, width, depth, and time. She believes God to be close by, perhaps in other dimensions that our current eyes cannot detect. Near, but hidden. She said, "When we die, we cross over into another dimension. I believe that there are many different levels over there, some higher and some lower. I also believe that when we get there, our friends, loved ones and yes, even our pets that have passed on are there to greet us. I believe that we will watch the life we lived."

Mary Griffin connects the joys of today with the joys of the future. "I think of my most treasured memories and happiest moments: my wedding day, the birth of my children, family gatherings, birthday parties, time with friends, snuggling with my husband, rocking my babies, Christmas mornings with the kids, watching the sunrise."

Marie Boswell envisions a tangible future for eternity: "beautiful flowers, bushes and trees…this is what heaven will be—right here on this beautiful planet, with clouds of many colors, stars, moon, sun and rainbows, rivers, oceans, butterflies…Beautiful people with joy, smiles and love on each face. Laughter, listening and enjoying each other. Beautiful music and singing. Happy conversation. Clean air and using our gifts and talents by giving them to each other. No more pain. Walking, flying, running, and doing everything we have always wanted to do."

William Newman has a common misconception that pictures a dull, boring, unattractive Christian future, "sitting on a cloud strumming a harp. I've never heard of a description of the Christian heaven that sounded like any place I'd like to spend eternity."

Herein lies the problem. Satan has successfully robbed us of the true picture of heaven's wonder and splendor. But I'll talk more in a later chapter about Satan's efforts in this area.

Finally, Lisa Hargrave believes, "… we will be given our glorified bodies, which will reign with him eternally in the new heaven and new earth."

Do You Doubt The Truth Of Scripture?

For some reason, most Christians believe in the virgin birth, the parting of the Red Sea, a giant named Goliath, that Jesus walked on water, and a talking snake in the garden of Eden, but throw in the towel at the mention of a six-day creation. Why is that?

A later chapter will outline Satan's strategy to undermine the words of God, but I believe this to be the case in Genesis 1. If Satan can get us to doubt Genesis 1, then it's much easier to get us to doubt Genesis 2, 3, and on to Revelation 21 and 22. Makes sense, doesn't it?

Bible Lectureship Surprise

A few years ago, I was a speaker on the program at a Bible lectureship. My topic was "iPod Evangelism." After I finished my presentation, I was excited to stick around and hear some of the other speakers. I was very interested to hear the first speaker when the introduction included a hardy appeal that he would end up as a professor at that university, but I was shocked that during the lesson—which was not on the subject of creation—he made fun of those who believed in a literal, seven-day creation week.

I listened with interest to the rest of the presentation, which I enjoyed, and at the end politely asked the speaker what verses he used to support the idea that a seven-day creation week was laughable. He was ready with an answer. He reached for his open Bible and read an underlined passage to me: "Here's one example right here," he began. The verse he read from used the simple phrase, "In my father's day." Then he was quick to make his point. He proceeded with the lecture as if I was just another student. He was polished and rehearsed. "Now that word for 'day' in the Hebrew is 'yom,' and this is certainly not a normal, twenty-four-hour day."

"Absolutely," I responded, "I agree. Now can you show me a verse that says the sun went down, and the sun came back up, and it's not a twenty-four-hour day?"

At this, he went ballistic. "Oh, I see you're a literalist," he barked. "We're not going to be able to talk." I was open to discussion, but he wasn't.

Immediately to my right, the man who had made the introduction at the beginning of the lecture jumped right into the conversation, although I had not addressed him. "You're going to focus on that and miss God," he almost yelled.

I bowed my head and began backing up, trying my best to talk softly and keep my cool. "I'm very sorry to have upset you, and I'm not talking about missing God, but believing God means what he says. Pardon me for upsetting you." I left distraught, discouraged, sad, and a little depressed.

Is the subject not even open to discussion among Christians anymore? If he had been open to dialogue, I would have asked him to consider some of the following ideas that reinforce the possibility that the days in Genesis 1 might be normal, ordinary days.

My Trip to New York City

If I took a trip to New York City and sent you a postcard that said, "We have been here for three days. We enjoyed a beautiful sunset each day as we looked out over the bay, and rose before the sun came up each morning to be able to see as many sights as possible," how long would you think I'd been there? Would you think I'd been there for millions of years, thousands of years, or three days? Many like to point out that a day to the LORD is like a thousand years, but I could say my trip to see the sights of New York was like a flash; it was a whirlwind tour and then we had to come home. Does that negate the fact that it was actually three days? No. Does anyone think Jonah may have been in the big fish for three thousand years? Why not apply that thousand-year thing to him?

The Best Commentary on Genesis 1

The best commentary on Genesis 1 is the Bible. The best way to understand a difficult passage is to try to locate other passages giving insight or somehow shedding light on that passage.

God states twice in the book of Exodus that He created the world in six days. (Exodus 20:8-11, & 31:16-17)

It's important to note here that the context surrounding this Exodus 20 reference is the giving of the Ten Commandments. All the other commandments are simply stated in matter-of-fact fashion. God said not to put other gods before him, not to make a graven image, not to take his name in vain, not to murder or commit adultery, not to steal, bear false witness, or covet, and to be sure to honor our fathers and mothers, but on one commandment, and only one commandment, he tells us why. Remember the Sabbath, because he wanted them to rest after six days of work just like he had rested after his six days of work.

The whole world operates with a seven-day week. God invented the seven-day week. God made it clear that the seven-day week is patterned after the seven-day creation week. Period. Why don't we accept that with the same child-like faith it takes to believe fire came from heaven to destroy Sodom and Gomorrah? Do we question whether we should work six thousand years and rest for a thousand, or whether the forty years that Israel spent wandering in the desert was really just forty days? Doesn't make sense, does it?

Hebrew Writing Style Dictates Fact Rather Than Poetry

There used to be a bumper sticker going around that stated simply, "God said it, I believe it, that settles it." But I think it would be more accurate if it had read, "God said it, that settles it, whether I believe it or not!"

In a magazine article for *Answers Magazine*, Volume 4 Issue 1, Dr. C. Taylor, Hebrew linguistic expert, points out that it's not impossible to know if Genesis 1 is factual or symbolic in nature. He explains that there are two distinct styles of Hebrew writing. One is poetic and the other is a narrative, completely factual style. You can know by the style whether it's actually factual or not. Genesis 1 is written in the narrative, factual style, and since both styles exist, this speaks volumes about the nature of the information there. It's fact.

Jesus Gives His Opinion About the Creation Week

Did you know that Jesus weighed in with his opinion about the length of time between the creation and the murder of Abel? Surprised? I was when I found it. It comes from Luke 11:49-51. Jesus doesn't think there might be millions of years, or even thousands of years for that matter, between creation and the murder of Abel. He considered Abel's murder to be virtually synonymous with creation.

In a discussion about marriage and divorce in Mark 10:6, Jesus goes even further to confirm that Adam and Eve were created at the beginning of creation. This would leave no room for million-year days or thousand-year days in Genesis 1.

Did Adam Have A Belly Button?

Let's talk about Adam's belly button. Did he have one? In studying this interesting question, we actually discover the answer to an age-old question: "Which came first, the chicken or the egg?"

When God created the chicken and Adam named it a chicken, was it an egg, or was it a full-grown, fat, healthy yard bird? I think the answer's obvious—it was a full-grown male and female pair ready to peck for grain, lay eggs, and hatch more little chickens. Had to be. There was no other chicken to hatch the egg.

Likewise, Adam probably didn't have a belly button. Why? A belly button is a tie to your earthly mother through the umbilical cord. Adam had no earthly mother. He had a Creator—God. God made him out of the dirt he had already made. As a side note, evolutionists also take a position of faith: they also have faith that man came from dirt. They just think the dirt was magically already here, and that the dirt was mixed with water, making a primordial soup, and that somehow lightning or electricity charged the dirt and caused life to form and evolve. Either story requires faith; I just happen to believe that the evolutionists have an unfounded faith, since this cannot be duplicated scientifically.

Now let's take this discovery further. Did trees in the Garden of Eden have rings? Good question. We don't know for sure, but I would say "probably." Why? Just as the chicken had muscle and bones, and just as Adam and Eve had all the necessary attributes to reproduce more people, I believe that trees probably had rings. I believe that the mountains and hills that God created also had layers of rock formations that would look like old mountains.

What Does the Fossil Record Prove?

Many Christians believe God did create everything, but also believe in millions or billions of years because science points to the fossil record to validate this theory. They use their special knowledge in this field and their special testing methods to prove that the rock formations are millions or billions of years old.

One problem is that their numbers keep changing as their testing equipment evolves, but the biggest problem is that there's no way to test their tests. Nobody can know for sure. I guess you could say that it requires faith to believe in their tests and in their methods, and scientific faith should not contradict biblical revelation, but theirs often does because of what they place their faith in: potentially fallible dating methods. At this point, many scientists and geologists choose to have more faith in their experts and dating methods than they do in God's Holy Word.

The fossil record is used to prove there were millions of years, and millions of years are substantiated by the fossil record. This is called circular reasoning. The old earth theory teaches millions of years proven by the fossil record. But this would require millions of years of dead things immortalized in the fossil record before sin. God says death came after sin in the garden. Difficult to reconcile, isn't it?

Adam, the First Man, and Eve, Mother Of All People

Some try to say there were other men prior to Adam like Cro-magnum man, or men God created without souls who lived elsewhere around the planet, but this position cannot withstand the test of Scripture. 1 Corinthians 15:47 teaches us that Adam was the first man, and Genesis 3:30 teaches us that Eve was the mother of all people everywhere.

Death Entered Creation Through One Man

A child would never read thousands of years into Genesis 1. Where did that idea come from? The only logical place is from the theory of evolution. The only reason to call the Genesis 1 days thousands of years long is to make a way to fit evolution into creation, allowing time for one mutation after another. Sounds simple enough, so what's the problem? The problem is that this requires the death of each generation of developing species, and 1 Corinthians 15:20-21 teaches that death never occurred until after man sinned in the garden of Eden.

Some Christians believe that there could be millions of years in the creation week, but unless they think those millions of years can be death-free, that idea is a direct contradiction to Scripture. Notice that it does not say that death came to mankind through Adam, it says death came in the world through Adam. Plant death, animal death, all death. Period. This in itself is a strong argument against the theory that the creation week was millions or thousands of years.

Adam Lived To Age 930

Adam was created at the beginning (Mark 10:6). So if Adam lived just one day of the creation week and the days that week were thousand-year days, the very next day he would have been a thousand years old. But scripture dispels this by stating in Genesis 5:5 that Adam died at the ripe old age of nine hundred and thirty.

Science Versus Scripture on the Subject of Death

Science says death is a permanent part of history. Scripture says death is a temporary enemy that did not exist in the garden of Eden and will be destroyed permanently at an appointed time in the future: "The last enemy to be destroyed is death" (1 Corinthians 15:26, NLT).

Mount Rushmore

Mount Rushmore is beautiful. The work on Mount Rushmore began in 1927. Almost 400 workers were employed during the peak of the construction work there. Dynamite was used to remove larger portions of rock, and pneumatic drills were used to finish the work. The granite that was removed totaled 450,000 tons during the entire process. Many skilled drillers were employed, and a high skill level was required. A model had been constructed, and this was used to project measurements that calculated where to drill holes for the dynamite and how deep to go. The end result is a thing of beauty, attracting thousands of visitors every year. It's quite a sight to see.

Would anyone in his right mind believe that the intricate beauties of the faces carved onto Mount Rushmore were created randomly by wind and rain erosion? Of course not. And Mount Rushmore is an inanimate object. It doesn't live, breathe, move, function, or think. Yet we sit there, mesmerized when Discovery Channel matter-of-factly informs our impressionable children that man evolved from primordial soup shocked with a lightning bolt and don't even raise an objection. What's wrong with this picture? It leaves out the truth. It leaves out God, true Creator of everything, according to Genesis 1.

Boeing 747

A Boeing 747 is a complicated creation, but not nearly as complicated as a human body, so let's consider an evolutionary theory for this airplane as opposed to a designer theory.

If we put all the parts of a Boeing 747 in a room with a bomb and detonated the bomb, how many millions of years of explosions with the right parts present would it take before one explosion caused the parts to end up in exactly the right places? Or, to be fair, let's say we lengthened the experiment to billions of years—how many explosions would it take?

Ridiculous, isn't it? It never would, would it? Yet we readily accept this as a possibility with the human body? No way.

Big Bang Has Serious Flaws

Big Bang is a massive explosion. Do explosions usually bring order, or chaos? Explosions bring chaos. Big Bang says the sun was formed before the earth. Genesis 1:1 and verses 16-19 state that the earth was formed before the sun. Some say you can believe the Bible and Big Bang, but these two positions are direct opposites in this critical area.

In addition, the laws of science correctly calculate that in an explosion, all things spin in the same direction. Over and over, the universe defies this pattern. Some planets orbit backwards. Some moons around some planets spin backwards by orbiting them in the opposite direction as the planet itself is spinning. True science proves Big Bang is a myth. Design requires a designer. God.

Patterns In The Universe

Have you ever noticed that from the smallest known objects—protons, neutrons, and electrons—to the largest solar systems that there is a pattern? Solar systems have planets rotating around a central point or object. Protons, neutrons, and electrons have parts rotating around a central point or object. Design reveals a designer. Design confirms a designer. God.

Don't Add to or Take Away From Scripture

Psalm 119:130, Proverbs 30:5-6, and Revelation 22:18-19 all provide dire warnings against adding to or taking away from scripture. God means business. Unless the context calls for a symbolic interpretation, consider it literal. We'll come back to that later in the prophecy section of this book.

Bible Genealogies Discourage
the Old Earth Theory

A friend of mine who goes on mission trips to Africa has encountered areas heavily populated with Muslims. Muslins already trust Abraham, and they consider Jesus a prophet. So when they discover that the Scriptures trace the genealogy of Jesus back to Abraham, many immediately trust him. And when they get to the book of John and see that the Word (Jesus) became flesh and dwelt among us, many are ready to become Christians. Biblical genealogies in Scripture that are dull and boring to many of us are the key to salvation for others. But there's also a connection between biblical genealogies and creation. If we can't trust the Bible to give accurate information about the genealogies that trace Jesus all the way back to Adam, then how can we trust the King for the assurance of forgiveness through Jesus, the last Adam: "One man, Adam brought death to many through his sin. But this other man, Jesus Christ, brought forgiveness to many through God's bountiful gift" (Romans 5:15-17, NLT). These two Adams are inextricably tied together for a divine purpose.

Biblical genealogies that are based on thousands of years rather than millions of years trace mankind from Adam to Noah, from Noah to Abraham, and on to David and Jesus. Adam was created at the beginning of creation. If the record of the genealogies is in doubt, then Christ is in doubt as the last Adam. And if the identity of Christ is in doubt, then his sacrifice for our salvation is in doubt. Be careful what you choose.

Scholars argue this issue and say there are gaps in these genealogies while others say there aren't. It's still a faith issue. I believe God said it, so that settles it!

Apparent Discrepancies in the Creation Theory

Some discount the possibility that the days of creation could have been normal days because there was no sun or moon until the fourth day. But consider this possibility. God is light, according to 1 John 1:5 and Isaiah 60:19-20, which say that God will be the light in eternity; the sun won't be needed.

If God can be our sun in eternity, couldn't he have been the sun so there could have been ordinary days in Genesis 1 that spanned the normal time? Don't normal days have evenings and mornings? Would you have believed it if God had said, "It was an ordinary day"? Isn't that what he's trying to say to us when he says there was evening (singular) and morning (singular)? How else would he confirm it? Again, he invented language, so don't you think he probably got the language right?

The Bible Is History: His Story

Do not forget that the Bible is a book of history, and it's also his story, God's story. It speaks of earthly things and heavenly things. In John 3, Jesus makes a point that if we doubt what Scripture says about earthly things like creation, there is no need to even discuss heavenly things like resurrection or heaven:

"I have spoken to you of earthly things and you do not believe; how then will you believe if I speak of heavenly things?" (John 3:12, NIV).

This is why I felt it necessary to begin by first asking you to consider your own position on whether it's a book of literal truth or not. If we cannot consider the Holy Scripture to be the literal truth that God made the world just like he said he did, that a worldwide flood saved one family and destroyed all others, that a virgin Jewish girl became pregnant by the Holy Spirit, and that this child died for you and literally rose from the grave, then we can never really look forward to rising from our own graves or living forever with him. It's all undeniably connected, and when you think you can simply unravel the parts you're having trouble believing, the unfortunate truth is that it all comes unraveled.

The Bible Declares Itself Literal

At the end of the beatitudes in Matthew 5, Jesus makes quite a startling statement. John MacArthur's Bible Commentary says it best:

> Here Christ emphasizes both the inspiration and the enduring authority of all Scripture. He specifically affirms the utter inerrancy and absolute authority of the OT as the Word of God – down to the least jot and tittle. ... Not one jot or tittle is thereby erased; the underlying truths of those Scriptures remain ... A 'jot' refers to the smallest Hebrew letter, the 'yohd,' which

is a meager stroke of the pen, like an accent mark or an apostrophe. The 'tittle' is a tiny extension on a Hebrew letter, like the serif in modern typefaces.

Here is the quote MacArthur is discussing: "Do not think that I have come to abolish the Law or the Prophets; I have not come to abolish them but to fulfill them. I tell you the truth, until heaven and earth disappear, not the smallest letter, not the least stroke of a pen, will by any means disappear from the Law until everything is accomplished" (Matthew 5:17-18 NIV).

How will we know when it's all accomplished? We'll see it. And for those who are prone to think that this passage says that earth will be annihilated, notice that if that is what it means, then heaven will be annihilated too, since they are equated in the text.

A Thousand Years Is Like a Day to God

Many try to use this verse in 2 Peter 3:8-10—which says that a day to God is like a thousand years—to provide a commentary on Genesis 1 and the length of the creation days. There are several reasons this isn't appropriate.

First, the context of this passage is God's judgment, not creation. Second, a thousand years in this passage is simply being used as an analogy to say that just because judgment hasn't happened yet, it doesn't mean God won't judge. He is patient. Time has no meaning to God. He invented time. He wants more people to be saved before time expires. Third, this works both ways. By that I mean that those who want to somehow fit thousands of years into the first six days of creation are quick to cite the first half of the verse, "a day is like a thousand years," but they don't want to talk about the second half: "a thousand years is like a day." One just cancelled out the other, didn't it? Finally, and perhaps most importantly, it's inappropriate to use a Greek word in Greek context to provide commentary on a Hebrew word in the Hebrew context.

Yom Is the Hebrew Word for Day

As I wind down this discussion of the literal nature of Scripture and the reasons to consider the possibility that the days in Genesis 1 were normal days, one last point carries some significant weight. The word *day* in Hebrew is the word *yom*. But the word day doesn't always mean a twenty-four-hour day. Here's a sentence with the word day having three different meanings: "In my father's day, it took a day to cross the Sahara Desert during the day." The first day in that sentence means a period of time during Dad's youth, probably years. The second day means a twenty-four-hour period. And the last day meant during the daylight hours.

It's also important to note that the word yom is used in the Old Testament well over twenty thousand times. So how can anyone be so sure the uses in Genesis 1 are twenty-four-hour days? Every time in the Bible when the word yom is attached to a number (like a number of days) or the words evening or morning, it always means a twenty-four-hour day. The only passage where that's ever questioned is Genesis 1. And the only reason to question it is to introduce the possibility of millions or billions of years. It's probably best and most consistent to take it as it's written. A literal interpretation fits the context.

Preponderance of Evidence

I was once talking about Scripture to a man who thought he was a Bible expert. I immediately knew he wasn't when he stated flatly, "I know my Bible from Generations to Revolutions." My father-in-law, John Spencer, used to say about someone like this, "He doesn't know, and he doesn't know that he doesn't know."

I hope that the preponderance of the evidence presented here will overwhelmingly convince you that you can know God means what he says from Genesis 1 (Generations) to Revelation 22 (Revolutions).

What Might Be: A Tangible Heaven

"Hello, Jamie, I'm here to show you around a little bit today. Are you ready?"

"Where are we going?"

"You'll see. Let's go"

With those words, they instantly traveled to a beautiful valley at the base of a pleasant hill. Jamie looked around as the angel patiently waited for him to take in the new surroundings. They had traveled far.

"It's all too beautiful to be real. I'm still having a hard time believing I am really here, really seeing what's around me."

"Take your time. I understand completely. I have had the privilege of escorting many new arrivals over the centuries, and the wonder and newness that each person experiences are a joy to witness. Feel free to look around and enjoy the experience. There is no rush."

The valley was enormous. The flowers were thickly grouped patches exploding with color and smell. He'd never seen anything like it. Not only did words fail to convey the beauty, he now noticed that this place had an extra-dimensional quality about it that couldn't even be captured with a video camera. He asked his guide about it.

"I still feel a little disoriented by the way things appear. I can't even word my question right—things look thicker, deeper, more colorful. The smell of the flowers is fuller or stronger. The sky looks wider, heavier, deeper."

"I understand completely. I'll try to explain. But trust me, you'll get used to it. As you do, you'll notice from your viewing port of the post-flood earth that as you become more accustomed to your new environment, your previous home was simply an ugly, misshapen shadow of the real world. This world. You were accustomed to living in a four-dimensional world."

"Four-dimensional?"

"Yes. Length, width, depth, and time. Time was your fourth dimension, and it only moved in one direction. The King is preparing a place for you here where you will be allowed to observe and experience any part of the histories at your pleasure."

"What do you mean? What kind of place?"

"The best analogy I can offer for now is that it would be similar to your own past experience, like a trip to a movie theater. You will be able to observe any event from the histories, earth's past."

"But I thought we wouldn't even remember the things of earth. I thought if we had the memory of loved ones who didn't choose the LORD we would cry, and it said that there were no tears in heaven."

"Forgive me. Let me explain."

"The guidebook did not say that there would be no tears in heaven. You often sang a song that said that, but it's not in the Bible. Many songs were a poor reflection of the glory to come, though they meant well. The Scripture actually says that he will wipe away every tear. There must be tears in order for them to be wiped away.

If you had no access to the past, no memory of the minefield of life and how the King guided your navigation through it, no knowledge of how close you came to missing out on eternal life by the choices both you and others made each day, then the King, this place, and the whole process would be far less meaningful, less appreciated, less special, and most importantly, the King would be less glorified. In addition, you wouldn't even really be here; you would be someone else without the full knowledge and experiences you had on earth. The King didn't promise someone else an eternal life to replace you; he promised *you* eternal life!

"Eternal life isn't just a replacement for earth, it's a continuation of your existence that began upon conception in the shadow lands. Its full value and worth cannot be appreciated by beings who arrive here without complete memories of the sadness and despair that marked the temporary world, the fallen world."

"Wow, I do have lots to learn. I may be learning for decades."

"Learning never ceases! Let's move on. Please follow me ..."

Chapter 2: Prophecy Indications

"Jesus said, 'You're way off base, and here's why: One, you don't know your Bibles; two, you don't know how God works'"

(Mark 12:24, The Message).

Dad Was a Bible Scholar

When I was a little boy, Dad was preaching on weekends and coaching and teaching math during the week. Is it any wonder that math became my favorite subject? If you don't have someone around who can help you quickly see where you miss-added or misapplied a formula, math can be like Greek, but if you have someone to gently nudge you in the right direction to see your own mistake and then ask you a couple of questions to lead you to finding the right answer, then math can be elementary. Literally.

Dad was one of those gentle nudgers. He was good at gently nudging me in the right direction so I would be empowered to do more than just get tonight's homework assignment finished. With his help and nudging methods, I was much better prepared to go on to the next level in math because he helped me truly understand the basics. He was someone who teaches you to fish so you can eat fish for a lifetime instead of just handing you a stringer full for one good meal. His ways and mannerisms prepared me for a lifetime of fishing for men by his example, his love for others, and his encouragement. He had a bedside manner like an old frontier doctor who not only made you want to learn more but also helped you better understand what you had already learned.

One of the things I loved about Dad was how well he knew the Bible. It was great having someone close by who could answer just about every Bible question I could think of. But the best part was how he applied his knowledge by taking the time to share Jesus with others. As I was growing up, I remember that one night a week Dad was always gone. "Where's Daddy?" we'd ask Mom. She would gently remind us that this was Bible study night. He was over at so-and-so's house because they were interested in studying the Bible and they weren't Christians.

As I was growing up, it was a given that dads studied their Bibles so they could teach others about Jesus and God. Period. So I got in the habit.

Beginning Prayer

Lord, *I pray that my study in the area of prophecy will be a blessing to all who read this right now. As I am still growing in Christ, I pray that everyone deficient in using your knowledge of the future in bringing souls to Christ will use these insights to improve in that area. And even more than this, I pray that a better understanding of prophecy will open all eyes, ears, minds, and hearts to a deeper and more complete understanding of and excitement for heaven. In Jesus's name, Amen.*

The Beginnings of Evangelism

The Book of Acts records the three missionary journeys of the Apostle Paul. As I read through these, I noticed a pattern. When he got to a new town or village, he always went first to the same place to spread the gospel of Jesus Christ. He always went first to the Jewish synagogue. Why? I believe that there were at least two reasons. First, this was obedient to the command of Christ,

"To the Jew first, and also to the Greek." But the other reason has prophetic implications. Let's explore it together.

If Paul had begun with a non-Jewish audience, think how much more difficult it would have been to start a church in that city. He would begin his story by saying, "You know the Messiah that was supposed to come? He has come!"

The non-Jew would have responded, "No. What Messiah?" But the Jew would quickly respond, "Yes. He was to be a descendant of King David, from the tribe of Judah, born in Bethlehem," and on and on he would go.

In other words, by beginning with a Jewish audience Paul had a common starting point, background knowledge of the specific Bible predictions—prophecies—about the Messiah who was to come. It was much easier to convert people who shared a common background, a common starting point. This gave him a huge advantage in spreading the gospel message from town to town. As a core group of Jews accepted his message about Jesus, they were able to spread the gospel much quicker than if they hadn't had that common ground. This was an ingenious plan: convert the Jew first, who was open to Christian evangelism because of being familiar with the ancient prophecies about the Messiah, then use these local Jews in each city, who had customers, friends, and acquaintances all over town, would spread the gospel message throughout the community. And it worked. The church flourished, in spite of the stiff Roman opposition.

What I Hope You'll See

Although a biblical study of heaven is not something we must all agree on, wouldn't it be worth it if the scriptural glimpses of heaven revealed in the Bible end up getting us excited about evangelism? That is my hope and prayer.

From the prophetic standpoint, here's what I hope this chapter will help you see: God made sure the first coming prophecies were all fulfilled literally. If the first coming prophecies are universally literal, doesn't that speak volumes concerning the second coming ones? And there are about three times as many predictions about the second coming as there are concerning the first. God's pattern is understandable, undeniable, traceable, and predictable. After considering the ideas put forth in this chapter, I think you'll see that it's likely that the second coming prophecies are just as real and literal as the first coming prophecies, or any promise of God, for that matter.

But it's not a salvation issue, and you must decide for yourself. Please just pray about it. And don't just take my word for it; study for yourself.

Prophecy Patterns in the Gospels

Have you ever noticed when you read through the gospels how often it says, "This happened to fulfill prophecy," and how it often even quotes the Old Testament prophecy right there with it? This pattern is repeated over and over.

One of the things I noted was that if the fulfillment hadn't been blatantly pointed out in Matthew, Mark, Luke, or John as the fulfillment of a particular prediction, we would never have made the connection on our own.

But as I read through these and started really meditating on them, a new question came to mind, one I never found the answer to in the many books on prophecy I read. I said to myself, *I wonder how many of these prophecies are symbolic and how many are actually literal.* So I set out to discover the answer. I took a green highlighter and began marking all the verses with fulfilled prophecies in Matthew, and I didn't stop until I had finished the gospel of John. And believe me, I was shocked at the answer. I think you will be, too.

Some of the prophecies discussed in the pages of the gospels included symbolism like the phrase "led as a lamb to slaughter." This lamb is a symbol of Jesus Christ, but this didn't negate the fact that he was literally slaughtered for our sins. The shocking reality that in many ways rocked my religious theology was that these ancient predictions about Jesus were one hundred percent literal. One hundred percent. Wow.

In fact, I actually counted the verses, and the volume of verses dealing directly or indirectly with prophecy were staggering. Matthew and Mark are approximately forty percent prophetic, Luke is approximately forty-eight percent, and John is fifty-four percent. I had heard and read that about a third of Scripture is prophetic but didn't have a clue that the gospels were so overwhelmingly so. And on top of all that, I had now discovered that the prophecies about the first coming of Jesus were one hundred percent literal. This stunning reality was almost more than I could fathom, but I had no choice. It was biblical fact.

Challenge

Every prophecy about the first coming of Jesus turned out to be literal. Messiah was to be born of a virgin, born in Bethlehem, called a Nazarene, and called out of Egypt. He was to bring healing and fill Galilee with glory. He was also to be betrayed by a friend by thirty pieces of silver, mocked and spat upon, rejected by his own, be wounded and die for our sins, and be buried in a rich man's tomb. Not a bone was to be broken, his clothing would be gambled for, and he was to have his hands and feet pierced. He was to rise in three days—the sign of Jonah. He was to be rejected, but then become the cornerstone of the church. I couldn't find a single prophecy that was only symbolic. Not one. Maybe you can, but I couldn't. For me, this will be a difficult pill to swallow.

What Does This Pattern Teach?

In Mark 12:24, Jesus chastises the Pharisees for not recognizing the patterns of how God works. Since we now have the entire

Bible at our disposal, I believe we are just as responsible for recognizing those patterns. We have God's prophecy pattern in Scripture to evaluate and learn from. He made sure the first coming prophecies were all fulfilled in a literal fashion. And remember, some of them appeared to be contradictory or mutually exclusive in nature. Let me illustrate.

The Messiah was to be born in Bethlehem, called a Nazarene, and called out of Egypt. Some said that these couldn't all three be literal. The Messiah was to be born in Bethlehem, but he would also be called a Nazarene, some reasoned, by taking the Nazarite vow and follow the rules and regulations that went with it. In addition, since the Messiah was to be called out of Egypt, this would be fulfilled symbolically since he was a descendant of those who were called out of Egyptian slavery many generations before.

God did it differently. God did it literally. Jesus was literally born in Bethlehem because Joseph and Mary were required to go there for the Roman census. Jesus was called a Nazarene because he literally grew up in Nazareth. And Jesus was literally called out of Egypt when the angel told Joseph in a dream that King Herod—who had been trying to kill Jesus—had died. Literal. All three.

Now here's the big question that you must ask for yourself, "If one hundred percent of the first coming prophecies came true literally, does this pattern reveal anything about the second coming prophecies?" Again, according to Jesus in Mark 12:24, the answer to this is a resounding, "Yes."

Christians Say the Old Testament Points to Jesus as Messiah

Many are unaware that the Bible reveals the purpose of prophecy. Revelation 19:10 says, "The essence of prophecy is to give a clear witness for Jesus" (NLT). Prophecy reveals Jesus as Messiah and Son of God, Savior of the world. That's its purpose.

As I pondered this, I thought about my trip to Israel a few years ago and remembered the attitude Jewish people have about Jesus. Christians point to passages like this one in Isaiah and say, "See, those are the names for Jesus: Wonderful Counselor, Mighty God, Everlasting Father, and Prince of Peace."

"For a child is born to us, a son is given to us. And the government will rest on his shoulders. These will be his royal titles: Wonderful Counselor, Mighty God, Everlasting Father, Prince of Peace. His ever expanding, peaceful government will never end. He will rule forever with fairness and justice from the throne of his ancestor David. The passionate commitment of the LORD Almighty will guarantee this!" (Isaiah 9:6, NLT).

The Orthodox Jew, an expert in Old Testament Scripture replies calmly, "At what point was the government on the shoulders of Jesus of Nazareth? The prophets tell us that Messiah will sit on the throne of David. When did that happen? Messiah was to bring peace. Since Jesus came onto the scene has there been peace? If you say yes, it's a simple thing for me to refute this by pointing to the World Wars, the Holocaust, and countless other battles since that time. Messiah was to bring healing to all his people. While you may point to a few so-called miracles of healings that some claim occurred around Jesus, I ask, do you ever get sick? Do Christians get cancer? Do devout followers of Jesus have all kinds of diseases? This will not be the trademark of Messiah. You are mistaken about Jesus of Nazareth."

As a Christian, how would you respond to this? Remember, the biblical test for a true prophet was one hundred percent fulfillment. Does Jesus's ministry or does Christianity in general pass this test? No. Do church members—phase one of the kingdom—ever get sick or die? Yes.

Am I saying the Orthodox Jew is right about Jesus? No. I'm just trying to get you to think about overcoming his objection, leading him to Jesus, and opening his eyes to the fact that their Messiah and our Jesus are one and the same because there are two comings. The New Testament records the first one. There is still a second one. The first one offered glimpses of the complete story. The King of kings and Lord of lords will come and rule from David's throne as the world government rests on His shoulders. His ever-expanding, peaceful government will never end. He will rule forever with fairness and justice from that throne. And it's interesting to check out the first sermon in Acts 2 to see the location of David's throne; surprisingly, it's not in heaven.

Key Verses

There are a couple of key verses that shed some interesting light in this area of prophecy. One is at the end of Luke, and the other is at the beginning of Acts.

> Then the two from Emmaus told their story of how Jesus had appeared to them as they were walking along the road, and how they had recognized him as he was breaking the bread. And just as they were telling about it, Jesus himself was suddenly standing there among them. "Peace be with you," he said. But the whole group was startled and frightened, thinking they were seeing a ghost! "Why are you frightened?" he asked. "Why are your hearts filled with doubt? Look at my hands. Look at my feet. You can see that it's really me. Touch me and make sure that I am not a ghost, because ghosts don't have bodies, as you see that I do."
>
> Luke 24:35-39 (NLT)

Jesus was quick to point out that his resurrection body had physical qualities. He was not just an ethereal, see-through, spiritual being. He would later even invite Thomas to touch his side and feel his hands. His body, which was about to ascend up into the clouds, was tangible, real, and physical. Now notice the passage continues:

"As he spoke, he showed them his hands and his feet. Still they stood there in disbelief, filled with joy and wonder. Then he asked them, 'Do you have anything here to eat?' They gave him a piece of broiled fish, and he ate it as they watched" (Luke 24:40-43, NLT).

As if to further emphasize the normal, physical nature of his resurrected body, he asks for food and then consumes it in their presence. This act is given even more credence by the many passages that emphasize feasting in heaven.

Next we notice something very significant: "Then he said, 'When I was with you before, I told you that everything written about me in the law of Moses and the prophets and in the Psalms must be fulfilled' " (Luke 24:44, NLT).

What did he just say? That everything written about him in the Old Testament "must be fulfilled." Not that everything had been fulfilled, but that everything will be fulfilled. How do you think it will be fulfilled, symbolically or literally?

What Jesus Didn't Say

Sometimes, to get the full impact of what a passage teaches, we need to evaluate what is not said. Jesus had literally fulfilled every single prophecy about his first coming. Not some of them or even most. All. Note now that he didn't say, "Everything written about me in the law of Moses and the prophets has now come true." Why? Because they hadn't. The only ones that had come true were the first coming ones, and they were one hundred percent literal.

Even though he was walking around in a physical body, eating and drinking with his disciples, showing off his battle scars and preparing them for Pentecost and their upcoming worldwide mission, the prophetic Scriptures hadn't all come true. This reality is made even more confusing by the fact that many of the prophetic verses he is referring to have first coming fulfillments and second coming fulfillments mixed together!

Now let's look at the pivotal point in this passage: "Then he opened their minds to understand the Scriptures" (Luke 24:45, NLT).

What Just Happened to Them?

Keep in mind that this is the same group that throughout the ministry of Jesus kept missing the point. They argued over who was the greatest, they had to ask privately what Jesus meant when he told a parable, they wanted the children to leave Jesus alone, and they suggested he send the crowds away when it was suppertime. Over and over they missed the point.

That chapter in the disciples' lives—the chapter where they were constantly missing the point—was over. Never again would they ask an irrelevant question. Jesus changed all that. How? By opening their minds to correct understanding of and interpretation of the prophetic Scriptures about him.

Time was short, and Jesus knew he had to rapidly finish their training and give them a complete understanding of the Old Testament so they could face the huge task at hand, worldwide missions. They needed to be rock solid in their understanding of how he was the exact, literal fulfillment of the Old Testament predictions about the Messiah.

So what did Jesus do? I believe that in that instant, he made them prophecy experts. Prophetic passages were destined to help the world see that he was the long-awaited Messiah. They now had complete, divine understanding of how Jesus was the Messiah, and perfect clarity of how the Old Testament pointed directly to him as LORD and King.

How could it be any less? They were about to face a Jewish audience and Jewish authorities who knew how to dot every 'i' and cross every 't,' so they better be ready. So Jesus—in some supernatural way—got them ready, completely ready.

Having Eyes to See and Ears to Hear

A few years ago, I got in the habit of reading the Bible every day and then writing down a short prayer. When I started this habit, I was determined not to be upset at myself if I missed a day or two. I wanted this to be relaxing; not an additional source of pressure in my life. I wanted it to become my time of regular, real, daily communication with God. I wasn't really sure how it would go, where it would go, or even if it would ever go anywhere, I just knew I wanted to do it.

A variety of life's ups and downs, worries and fears, and daily concerns are bound up in these many pages of prayer memories, and it's often very encouraging to review some of it and remember how highly concerned I was about something back then. Many of the issues I wrote about ended up being much less critical than I originally thought. This gives my boys—who will read every word some day after I've gone home—something meaningful and tangible to meditate on and hopefully grow from. So I'm happy for their sakes that I am doing it.

But something else began happening on a regular basis that came as a big surprise to someone like me, someone who thought God was actively involved in people's daily lives in Scripture but found it a little difficult to imagine that sort of thing still happening today. I could probably give you hundreds of examples, but let me focus on seeing a truth in the inerrant pages of God's Holy Word that I never saw before, although it has been there all along, something that even many dedicated, scholarly men have missed. Here's what happened.

During this particular time frame, I had been in the habit of reading a passage and then writing down my prayer. I would put the date, the day of the week, and the time of day. But this particular day—for no apparent reason—I decided to reverse the order and wrote down my prayer first.

For some reason—the Holy Spirit—it popped into my mind that many passages in the Bible pointed out that the people of God didn't have eyes to see or ears to hear what was truly going on around them, what God was busy doing. Immediately, I decided that this would be my prayer that day, and I began to write, "Lord, give me eyes to see and ears to hear where you are at work around me and the things you are doing so I can join into the work you are focused on. In Jesus's name, Amen."

Then I opened my Bible to read the passage I was scheduled to read that day. I had been in the process of reading the Bible through on a one-year program, and I began reading in Deuteronomy 29. The words on the page blew me away, and it could not have been an accident that I had prayed that prayer and then read these words:

> Moses summoned all the Israelites and said to them, "You have seen with your own eyes everything the Lord did in the land of Egypt to Pharaoh and to all his servants and to his whole country—all the great tests of strength, the miraculous signs, and the amazing wonders. But to this day the Lord has not given you minds that understand, nor eyes that see, nor ears that hear!"
>
> Deuteronomy 29:2-4 (NLT)

These people had seen many miracles and supernatural acts that could not be explained in earthly terms, yet they complained daily about what God didn't do instead of focusing and praising him for all the things he did do: plagues on their enemies, deliverance from death, daily manna, quail, and water from a rock.

Then it dawned on me: having eyes to see and ears to hear is a gift from God. We need to desire it enough to ask God for it. And that's just what I'd done. Then I also noticed a cross-reference from Proverbs that confirmed it: "Ears to hear and eyes to see—both are gifts from the Lord" (Proverbs 20:12, NLT).

Returning to Luke 24

I also took the time to cross-reference this pivotal verse in Luke 24 and came up with some interesting discoveries. While the New Living Translation says that he opened their minds to understand the Scriptures, several other translations use some other insightful words. The Message states that, "He went on to open their understanding of the Word of God, showing them how to read their Bibles this way." The New King James version says he opened their comprehension of the Scriptures. The Complete Jewish Bible offers an interesting twist by connecting the Tanakh—the Jewish term for the Old Testament. Simply stated, this means that Jesus opened their minds so they could understand the Old Testament. Young's Literal Translation says he enabled them to understand the "writings." The Bible in Basic English states that he made the writings clear to their minds.

The Amplified Bible adds the word "thoroughly," as it says that Jesus opened their minds to understand the Scriptures. What Scriptures? The prophetic Scriptures. He is telling them that the truth about his comings was in the ancient prophetic writings all along. God still never does anything without first revealing it to his servants, the prophets (Amos 3:7). He intended to suffer and die. He came to be the literal fulfillment of all the predictions.

Now add to this the fact that he says everything written about him in the law and the prophets must come true. He did not say that it had come true, but that is must come true.

With that backdrop, let's look at the second important passage.

After Forty Days Discussing Heaven, They Just Had One Question

I've got a question for you. If you had the opportunity to ask Jesus just one question before he left you, what would it be? Would it be about your loved ones? Would it be about your own salvation? Would it be about your own future, how you would die, or what decisions you should make on some big issue in your life?

Let's make it a little more complicated. What if you were allowed to hear Jesus lecture to you for forty days—on the subject of his choice—right before he left, and then you could ask your one question? Would the subject he chose change the question you asked? It would mine. If he had just focused on one primary topic for forty days and then let me ask my one question, I would ask a question that related to the subject. Wouldn't you?

When people are dying, if they are able to talk just prior to their death, what would you think they would talk about? Would they be focused on their financial picture, their net worth, or their success in their career? No, not usually. When we face death, we are usually focused on the things that mean the most.

Jesus was about to ascend to heaven so the Holy Spirit could come. He spent forty days discussing one main topic, knowing he was about to leave for thousands of years before returning. What did he focus on? According to Acts 1:3-7, his dissertation was all related to just one subject: heaven.

Based on the knowledge that their minds had been opened in a supernatural way to a complete and accurate understanding of the Old Testament prophecies about Jesus and the kingdom, coupled with the fact that the King of kings had just spent forty days discussing heaven, I believe it would be irresponsible and untrue to say that this was an irrelevant question.

One thing we can say for sure: as Jesus discussed the kingdom of God for a full forty days, he didn't say one thing to dispel the notion that Israel would be restored to a place of honor and greatness in the world and in God's sight. Furthermore, notice that the answer Jesus gave focused on the timing instead of the reality of this subject. "The Father alone has the authority to set those dates and times." What a great opportunity for him to dispel the notion of an earthly, physical kingdom once and for all. He could have done this by saying, "Guys, you just don't get it! There won't be an earthly kingdom." But he doesn't do that, does he? When you stop and think about it, he actually affirms this assertion by revealing that God alone knows the *timing* of it.

Matthew 24: Past or Future?

Many years ago, I was teaching a Bible class and did an overview of all the different eschatological viewpoints concerning the end times. After the class had been growing rapidly over the first month or so, an elderly gentleman came by my office to talk to me about Matthew 24.

"Steve," he said, "Matthew 24 is all history. It happened in 70 A. D."

"All right," I replied. "Let's read it together."

We sat side by side, and I began at verse one, reading it out loud. Then we got down to these verses:

> "The day is coming when you will see what Daniel the prophet spoke about—the sacrilegious object that causes desecration standing in the Holy Place. [Reader, pay attention!] Then those in Judea must flee to the hills. A person out on the deck of a roof must not go down into the house to pack. A person out in the field must not return even to get a coat. How terrible it will be for pregnant women and for nursing mothers in those days. And pray that your flight will not be in winter or on the Sabbath. For there will be greater anguish than at any

time since the world began. And it will never be so great again. In fact, unless that time of calamity is shortened, not a single person will survive. But it will be shortened for the sake of God's chosen ones."

Matthew 24:15-22 (NLT)

Now he had a problem. Many people fail to realize that prophecies in Scripture often have a double fulfillment: a "near" fulfillment and a "far" fulfillment. Parts of the prophecy can easily be pointed to in history and seen as having been at least partially fulfilled, but then phrases and sections often appear that cannot have fulfillment in the past, so it must be a future event. This particular passage is one of the better examples of this. The Holy Place was definitely desecrated when Rome conquered Jerusalem, Christian Jews did flee the area into the hills, and it was a time of great horror. So we definitely see some fulfillment in what happened in Jerusalem in 70 A. D. But we do not see the complete and ultimate fulfillment. Not even close. Let's start with the last one first.

Scripture says in verse 21 that this would be a greater time of anguish than at any time since the world began and that this calamity also surpasses all futures ones. In fact, verse 22 goes so far as to say that unless this terrible time was shortened by God's mercy, the entire human race was at risk. Some versions say that no flesh would be saved, while others say that all humans would be killed, but the meaning is the same: mankind would be wiped out if God didn't intervene. One possible scenario for this would be a nuclear holocaust.

After reading this part, I turned to my elderly friend and said, "Although 70 A. D. was a terrible time of slaughter for the Jews by the powerful Roman army, the whole human race was not at risk. Now let's look at the next few verses."

Verses 29-31 revealed that immediately after this period, the sun and moon would become dark, stars would fall from the sky, the powers of heaven would be shaken, and Jesus would show up to gather his own.

Now my friend had an additional set of problems bursting his bubble and destroying his thinking that Matthew 24 was all history: the sun is still shining, the moon is still lighting up the night, and the stars are still in the sky. At this point, it was obvious that Matthew 24 was not all history. The man gently excused himself with, "I will study that and get back to you."

That was years ago, and I never heard from him about it again. That didn't mean he was convinced he was wrong, just in retreat or denial. I don't always like what the Word says, but I accept it, often in spite of what I was taught on the subject by other fallible humans, who may have been wrong.

Conclusion to Consider

God made sure the first-coming prophecies were all fulfilled literally, and there are about three times as many prophecies about the second coming than there are concerning the first. His pattern is understandable, undeniable, traceable, and predictable. And I predict the second-coming prophecies are just as real and literal as the first-coming prophecies, or any promise of God for that matter.

But it's not a salvation issue, and you must decide for yourself. Please pray about it. And don't just take my word for it; study for yourself.

What Might Be: Being in Covenant with God

"Welcome, Jamie. Are you ready for your training today?"

"Yes, absolutely! I am amazed at how my new understanding of Scripture is making all of history come to life in new and wonderful ways. And I am overwhelmed at how this knowledge enhances my real life here with all of you and the King."

"You have only just begun, but I admit that I am pleased at your progress and at your interest in learning. The King blesses you image-bearers in a special way with his nature, his creativity, his power, and his love, and we in the host never tire of witnessing the excitement in your face or the thrill in your voice. We were created to witness and serve, both the King and the saved, but you were created in his likeness.

"Today's lesson concerns prophecy."

"Prophecy? Okay, but why should I be concerned about that now? I never really studied much in that area on earth. It never really seemed relevant. It seemed useless, a waste of time, almost fictional, or at the very least, so confusing that it wasn't really valuable."

"Yes, we watched how you focused on many other areas of Scripture. And you weren't the only one. Few Christians, less than 5 percent in fact, realize the tremendous value that the King places on this vital subject.

"Prophecy is extremely important in the opinion of the King. In fact, the Bible is almost forty percent prophetic in nature, and few notice that they are literally discounting or minimizing this all-important topic by taking the attitude you just described. Only the King knows the future, and prophecy is his method of validating the truth of the Bible. By discounting prophecy, you were unknowingly causing a significant part of the Scripture to be devalued. We have watched this cause him sadness many times over the centuries.

"As Revelation 19 states, the essence of prophecy is witnessing for Jesus Christ as Messiah and Savior and for convincing the world of his true identity. Although you were completely unaware of its power, prophecy is actually the reason for the conversion of many souls. God knows the future in detail and he uses all things to reveal himself. Part of that revelation is how we join the kingdom and walk in his power. This reality brought many people to faith, the cause of what has mushroomed into an uncountable multitude of people who will live forever in this world, the real world. "

"I preached baptism! I believe in the vital importance of it and was disappointed that many good, religious people I knew minimized the importance of it."

"Yes, Jamie, I know. And baptism is important, even necessary, but you never truly understood why."

"What do you mean?"

"In order to help you understand why it was included, you need to have a more complete understanding of how the Father always chose to work in a covenant relationship. It was his way, his law, his method of forming alliance, friendship, and relationship.

"When God told Abraham about all the blessings he would receive through his descendants, Abraham had no descendants. So he turned to God and asked him how he could know that God would do all he said he would. The Father simply instructed him to go get a heifer.

"The ancient ritual of the covenant had a series of steps that were required. They were non-negotiable, known to all, and specific. The details were very similar to, but much more binding, than your understanding of contracts from your post-flood time period. Pay close attention as I explain the steps involved and as I review the significance of each requirement.

"First, there was an exchange of robes. The outer robe was seen as part of a man's identity. They would exchange robes to signify a confusion of identity. When men exchanged their robes and others saw them coming from afar, they would be confused about who was coming, because they first recognized the person by their unique outer garment. The New Testament equivalent of this act was similar, yet unique. Notice this passage from the New Covenant in Galatians:

> You are all sons of God through faith in Christ Jesus, for
> all of you who were baptized into Christ have clothed

yourselves with Christ. There is neither Jew nor Greek, slave nor free, male nor female, for you are all one in Christ Jesus. If you belong to Christ, then you are Abraham's seed, and heirs according to the promise.

Galatians 3:26-29 (NIV)

"Galatians teaches that baptism was the covenant act of putting on Christ, or clothing yourselves with Christ. Faith is the prerequisite that leads to baptism into Christ. Then they were to act like Christ would act in everything they did. If a doctor became a Christian, he was to act as Christ would act if he were a doctor. If a teacher, they were to show the world how Christ would act if he were a teacher. If a lawyer, a merchant, a magistrate, or any other professional became a Christian, they were to bring the fragrance of Christ to every situation, every circumstance, every difficulty. The world is always watching to see how Christians react to daily life. And the enemy is quick to point out the discrepancies when they occur. Your influence is more far reaching than any of you realize. And when your actions misrepresent the King, the clothing you are wearing— your identity as a follower of Christ—reflects poorly the King's intentions, disappointing him greatly. But when your responses are appropriate, this confusion of identity by the exchanging of your robes brings glory to the kingdom and joy to the King. As Galatians teaches, baptism is the identifying mark required for this identity exchange.

"The second requirement to being in covenant was the exchange of belts. Weapons were attached to the belt, so the belt itself was a symbol of strength. God pledged to provide his power and strength to overcome:

"Be strong in the LORD and in his mighty power.

Ephesians 6:10 (NLT)

He said to me, 'My grace is sufficient for you, for my power is made perfect in weakness.' Therefore I will boast all the more gladly about my weaknesses, so that Christ's power may rest on me.

2 Corinthians 12:9 (NIV)

"And, again, notice that baptism is connected to the power of being "in covenant" and having access to the power of God, the strength of wearing his belt:

"You were placed in the tomb with Christ through baptism. In baptism you were also brought back to life with Christ through faith in the power of God, who brought him back to life.

Colossians 2:12 (God's Word Translation)

We died and were buried with Christ by baptism. And just as Christ was raised from the dead by the glorious power of the Father, now we also may live new lives.

Romans 6:4 (NLT)

"The third step to being in covenant with God was the exchange of weapons. The exchange of weapons symbolized the exchange of enemies. His enemy became our enemy, and our enemy became his. In the covenant relationship, covenant partners came to the aid of each other in the event of an attack. Who was God's enemy? Satan. Who was mankind's enemy? After the sin in the garden of God, it was death. So now mankind must defeat Satan, and God must defeat death. Notice these passages from the Guidebook:

"Your enemy the devil prowls around like a roaring lion looking for someone to devour.

1 Peter 5:8 (NIV)

Our struggle is not against flesh and blood, but against the rulers, against the authorities, against the powers of this dark world and against the spiritual forces of evil in the heavenly realms.

Ephesians 6:12 (NIV)

"God sent Jesus down to defeat our enemy, death. Notice the Christians' eventual victory over death is the resurrection:

Since death came through a man, the resurrection of the dead comes also through a man. For as in Adam all die, so in Christ all will be made alive.

1 Corinthians 15:21-22 (NIV)

When the trumpet sounds, those who have died will be raised to live forever. And we who are living will also be transformed. For our dying bodies must be transformed into bodies that will never die; our mortal bodies must be transformed into immortal bodies. Then, when our dying bodies have been transformed into bodies that will never die, this Scripture will be fulfilled: "Death is swallowed up in victory. O death, where is your victory? O death, where is your sting?" For sin is the sting that results in death, and the law gives sin its power. But thank God! He gives us victory over sin and death through our LORD Jesus Christ.

1 Corinthians 15:52-57 (NLT)

"And notice that baptism is the first step in our resurrection: 'Have you forgotten that when we were joined with Christ Jesus in baptism, we joined him in his death? For we died and were buried with Christ by baptism. And just as Christ was raised from the dead by the glorious power of the Father, now we also may live new lives. Since we have been united with him in his death, we will also be raised to life as he was.'

(Romans 6:3-5, NLT).

"The fourth step required to be "in covenant" with God was a sacrifice. The heifer died, and its blood was sacrificed as a part of the covenant. God has always required blood to cover sin and re-establish relationship. In Abraham's case, it was animal blood, but in the Christian's case, it's the blood of the Savior on the cross. Blood is needed to cover sin and be 'in covenant.' Keep in mind that Jesus was sinless, but still needed baptism. His cousin, John, performed the act, though reluctantly. Then the King freely gave His blood, as the Holy Spirit testifies: 'This is the one who came by water and blood—Jesus Christ. He did not come by water only, but by water and blood. And it is the Spirit who testifies, because the Spirit is the truth'

(1 John 5:6, NIV).

"So in order to be in covenant, God required a sacrifice and submission to water baptism. Since Jesus himself performed the covenant act of baptism before beginning his ministry, so should we. As water and blood flowed from the side of the Savior, water and blood makes us clean in God's sight and gives us the right to enter into his presence with a heart of faith: 'Let us go right into the presence of God with sincere hearts fully trusting him. For our guilty consciences have been sprinkled with Christ's blood to make us clean, and our bodies have been washed with pure water.'

(Hebrews 10:22, NLT).

"The fifth step needed for a covenant relationship was called the walk of death. After the heifer was cut into two halves, the covenant partners had to walk through the blood together. Baptism is the New Covenant walk of death: 'God waited patiently in the days of Noah while the ark was being built. In it only a few people, eight in all, were saved through water, and this water symbolizes baptism that now saves you also—not the removal of dirt from the body but the pledge of a good conscience toward God. It saves you by the resurrection of Jesus Christ, who has gone into heaven and is at God's right hand—with angels, authorities and powers in submission to him'

(1 Peter 3:20-22, NIV).

"The same floodwaters that purged the evil saved the good. Baptism is a copy of this unearthly event. It takes faith to be baptized, but one without the other is incomplete, as a covenant without the walk of death is incomplete. Man cannot live underwater, so the King chose to use this truth, this covenant act, done in faith, to seal our covenant relationship with him. It was always meant to be a symbolic act of relationship, not a point of contention. But, as you are well aware, Satan has nurtured and encouraged much hotheaded turmoil over this simple covenant act of submission.

"God has always chosen to reveal his purpose to those with childlike faith and hide the same truths from the spiritually arrogant. For those willing to accept it, Jesus placed the final nail in the coffin of the idea that baptism was irrelevant when he told Nicodemus that no one could enter heaven without being born of water and the Spirit. God sees this spiritual change in the heart of faith, and the water requirement is fulfilled in believer's baptism.

"The sixth covenant step was the mark on the body. This was usually done on the wrist. In some cultures today, some call themselves blood brothers after having gone through this ritual. In Africa and South America, some tribes added the practice of putting a dark substance to dye the cut into a permanent mark. The dye caused a permanent stain in the exact shape of the cut. This could be easily seen when they greeted each other with a wave. The wave was meant to reveal that they were in a covenant relationship and communicate the reality that if the other man chose to attack the man waving, he would also have to deal with those in covenant with him. Covenant partners shared enemies and were required to defend each other.

"In Abraham's case, the bodily mark that signified the covenant was the mark of circumcision. Without this covenant mark, Abraham would not have been in covenant with God. When Moses failed to circumcise his sons, God was so angry that he started to kill him, so his wife quickly performed circumcision on the boys, quelling God's anger. And in the case of the New Covenant, as Romans explains, a pure heart is seen as a circumcised heart in God's sight: 'True circumcision is not merely obeying the letter of the law; rather, it is a change of heart produced by God's Spirit. And a person with a changed heart seeks praise from God, not from people' (Romans 2:29, NLT). And remember, God took a mark on his own wrists by dying on a cross on a hill called Calvary.

"The seventh covenant step was a pronouncement of blessings and curses. The tradition was for the covenant partners to face each other and pronounce a blessing on the partner if they kept the covenant and a curse on them if they did not. They would be blessed as they came out, as they went in, as they rose up each day, and as they lay down each night. Their wives would be blessed with children, the work of their hands would be blessed, and all their oxen, donkeys, crops, and fields would also be blessed with abundance. In short, if they kept the covenant, their whole life would be blessed.

"But woe to the man who broke the covenant in any way. If he did not come to the aid of his covenant partner or violated the pact in any manner, a curse would be on him. He would be cursed as he came out, as he went in, as he rose up, and as he lay down. His wife would be cursed, her womb would be cursed, his work would be cursed, and all his possessions would be cursed. It was a fearful thing to break the covenant, for then all the covenant blessings would be gone, and all hope would be lost for that man's future.

"The New Covenant equivalent is found in several places:

"Why do you worry about clothes? See how the lilies of the field grow. They do not labor or spin. Yet I tell you that not even Solomon in all his splendor was dressed like one of these. If that is how God clothes the grass of the field, which is here today and tomorrow is thrown into the fire, will he not much more clothe you, O you of little faith? So do not worry, saying, "What shall we eat?" or "What shall we drink?" or "What shall we wear?" For the pagans run after all these things, and your heavenly Father knows that you need them. But seek first his kingdom and his righteousness, and all these things will be given to you as well.

Matthew 6:28-33 (NIV)

And this same God who takes care of me will supply all your needs from his glorious riches, which have been given to us in Christ Jesus.

Philippians 4:19 (NLT)

And since we are his children, we are his heirs. In fact, together with Christ we are heirs of God's glory. But if we are to share his glory, we must also share his suffering.

Romans 8:17 (NLT)

But Christ has rescued us from the curse pronounced by the law. When he was hung on the cross, he took upon himself the curse for our wrongdoing. For it is written in the Scriptures, "Cursed is everyone who is hung on a tree." Through Christ Jesus, God has blessed the Gentiles with the same blessing he promised to Abraham, so that we who are believers might receive the promised Holy Spirit through faith.

Galatians 3:13-14 (NLT)

"The eighth step was the covenant meal. In this part of the ritual, the covenant partners sat at a table with witnesses present and shared the meal, but the most significant part was when the covenant partners fed each other the first few bites. This ritual continued in many Western-culture weddings in your time, Jamie. Your marriage tradition had the bride and groom feed each other the first bite of wedding cake after the marriage covenant vows were taken. But in the ancient culture of Abraham, certain words were repeated by each covenant partner during this process. As they fed their new partner those first few morsels, they would say, 'As you take this sustenance into your body, so you are taking in our covenant to be a permanent part of your nature from now until the day you perish.'

"Jamie, since you were from a church family who practiced the weekly observance of the LORD's Supper, you will easily relate to and appreciate that the Supper of the LORD is the New Covenant equivalent: 'As they were eating, Jesus took some bread and blessed it. Then he broke it in pieces and gave it to the disciples, saying, "Take this and eat it, for this is my body." And he took a cup of wine and gave thanks to God for it. He gave it to them and said, "Each of you drink from it, for this is my blood, which confirms the covenant between God and his people. It is poured out as a sacrifice to forgive the sins of many. Mark my words—I will not drink wine again until the day I drink it new with you in my Father's kingdom" (Matthew 26:26-29, NLT).

"Although most earthlings overlooked the significance of this ritual and its connection to God by way of a covenant relationship, the host of heaven was well aware of it, and his last phrase didn't go unnoticed in our realm.

"After his resurrection and ascension, he took up his rightful position at the right hand of the Father on high. He is to remain there until the time of the final restoration of all things, according to Acts 3. His return to earth at the second coming will conquer death and assure that God's will, will be done on earth as it is now done in heaven. Then he will drink again with the disciples and all of his resurrected followers. What a feast that will be!"

"Wait, I'm confused. I taught my sons to change the words of that prayer from 'Thy kingdom come' to 'thy kingdom has come.'"

"Yes, Jamie, you did. Those of us involved in assuring your safety noticed that as we were standing watch over you. But your teachers did not understand completely, and their limited understanding kept you from making the best choice on this issue. You believed that the church was the complete fulfillment of that prayer. You weren't completely incorrect, but the church was only a flicker, only the beginning of the explosion of reality that the kingdom will bring with it. It was a charcoal sketch of the final masterpiece, a pen-and-ink of the full-color print. The church was the beginning, the mechanism used by the King to begin to re-conquer the domain stolen by Satan. Let me back up and explain the scope of the plan the King is in the process of executing.

"As you have taught from Ephesians 6 about the principalities and powers of the unseen world, we in the host have lived and breathed this reality. At creation, Satan, then called Lucifer, was part of the host. This was before he led the rebellion against the Father. A member of the host was stationed as protector over every region of the earth. Then when the rebellion exploded in our realm and one third of the host followed Lucifer's twisted and prideful scheme, some of these rebels were in charge of regions on the planet. Their desire to rule and be worshiped led to blood sacrifice, ritualistic devotion, and animistic blasphemy that the faithful host could not believe. Demons, or fallen angels, were present at the worship of every idol, accepting every blood sacrifice, reveling in and accepting the worship of the deceived humans. In fact, we didn't understand why the King would tolerate it rather than obliterate their kind from existence. But the King used their rebellion, used sin itself to reveal the true-hearted, those destined for salvation.

"Satan thought he had won a great victory, but the King was planning all along to use deception against the chief deceiver and offer all mankind a choice: good or evil. We finally realized that the choice was a necessary part of the process that separates the good from evil. Would you want a wife who had no choice but to marry you, or would you rather have a wife who chose you when she could have chosen anyone? True love sets the object of that love free, free to stay or to go. Otherwise, love is not present. It took us decades, centuries to finally understand it. But once we did, it all made sense. It was also true of our own race, the host. God didn't make us a robotic mass of unthinking puppets. He gave us a free will and a chance to choose. Most of us chose faithfulness to the King, but some chose Satan's way of rebellion. The King wanted us all to stay, but it was up to each individual. When Satan rebelled, each member of the host had to choose. Would they stay with the King or follow the silver-tongued leader of the rebellion?

"Again, Satan thought he was winning ground, but in this he was also deceived. Those of us in the host only understood bits and pieces of the King's overall plan at first, much like your thinking that the church was the ultimate fulfillment of the kingdom on earth. Then we started to put the pieces together and get the big picture.

"God's plans included letting Satan's rebellion occur, unsuppressed. This gave all mankind the chance to make a choice and reveal his position in relation to the King. Would they follow Satan, or would they stand with the faithful host and the Triune King? God was content to let Lucifer's deception deepen and allow much time to pass before the great restoration would begin. Acts 3 reveals that Jesus was to remain in heaven until the time for the final restoration of all things, and that is what he will do. He will restore all things. Complete restoration, worldwide perfection, it will be beautiful beyond description. Unless you have seen the original, perfect earth with your own eyes as we have, it is impossible to imagine. Eden.

"It is just as easy, perhaps easier, for the King to recreate what he once created, and that's exactly what he plans to do. He wants to walk with you, talk with you, and have continual, ongoing daily interaction. The King is all about relationship. And this goes far beyond what you know even now. As the Triune King has three unique parts, you are created in his image. You have three parts, too. You are body, soul, and spirit—uniquely so. Nothing else in all the rest of creation is so created. Although you are in a temporary body wearing temporary garments, your new body will integrate your original DNA at the great resurrection. Otherwise, there would be no need for the graves to open and the sea to give up their dead. And your new garments will adorn that body with perfection. You will wear your good deeds, your rewards for willingly choosing to serve the King of kings when you had a choice. You will reign with him on new earth for eternity. But that's a lesson for another day. Let me finish the covenant requirements for now. We still lack two steps.

"The ninth step required the exchange of names. I believe you remember this step, don't you, Jamie?"

"Yes. Abram became Abraham. And Sarai became Sarah."

"Correct, but do you know why?"

"I didn't know there had to be a reason."

"With the King, there is a reason for everything. Let me explain how it worked by giving you an example from your post-flood world that will enable you to understand.

"You normally signed your name 'Jamie Hemphill.' If you made a covenant with someone named 'Bill Smith,' your new name would be 'Jamie Smith Hemphill,' and his new name would be 'Bill Hemphill Smith.' And this would be permanent. A covenant relationship cannot be rescinded. This is what God did for Abram.

"God's name in the Hebrew is Yahweh. So he took the 'ah' from his own name and inserted it into Abram's and Sarai's. Now Abram was Abraham, and Sarai was Sarah. Then God took on Abraham's name by being called from then on in Scripture, 'The God of Abraham.'

"The New Covenant equivalent is quite simple in this case. When you gained enough faith to repent of your sins, confess Jesus as your LORD, and submit to baptism, you were called Christian. 'The disciples were called Christians first at Antioch' (Acts 11:26, NIV).

"But we in the host were surprised again when the Word—who became flesh to dwell on earth—used a special name for himself that also signified the covenant relationship: When he could have claimed relation to the deity he was by calling himself the Son of God, Jesus—in complete submission to covenant requirements—called himself the Son of Man. 'As Jonah was in the belly of the great fish for three days and three nights, so will the Son of Man be in the heart of the earth for three days and three nights.' (Matthew 12:40, NLT).

"Now we're ready for the final, and perhaps the most monumental step in the covenant relationship, the exchange of the oldest male child. In all ancient covenants, although foreign to your way of thinking, the covenant partners exchanged oldest male sons. Your son would go to live with your covenant partner as his son, and his son will become yours. Permanently. What a great sacrifice of commitment to the covenant it was to give up your first-born son for your covenant partner. In like manner, God asked Abraham to sacrifice Isaac, the son of promise, and then offered his own Son, Jesus, to die on the cross.

"The culmination was extravagant, but necessary, according to the King. Although we were allowed to stay the hand of Abraham as he wielded the knife to kill his son Isaac, we learned it was only because God knew that in his heart, Abraham had already killed the boy. Our confusion turned to joy.

"But when Jesus carried the cross to Golgotha, we were all close by, at the ready, prepared to stay the hands of the Roman soldiers in like manner, but we were prevented. Only then did we realize that the Son would actually be required to give up his physical life, if only temporarily. Only then did we understand the full impact of the prophecies. They were all completely literal. They were there to testify to the world for all the centuries to come that the King loves his people and that he means every word he says.

"Understanding flooded us, and excitement followed. If these predictions were so precise as to fulfill every one literally for the first coming, the same would be true for the second. Complete, planet-wide restoration for all creation was inevitable. Not only would mankind be resurrected and transformed into an eternal being, earth would be restored to its original beauty before finally being replaced with the permanent new earth.

> This is how much God loved the world: He gave his Son, his one and only Son. And this is why: so that no one need be destroyed; by believing in him, anyone can have a whole and lasting life. God didn't go to all the trouble of sending his Son merely to point an accusing finger, telling the world how bad it was. He came to help, to put the world right again. Anyone who trusts in him is acquitted; anyone who refuses to trust him has long since been under the death sentence without

knowing it. And why? Because of that person's failure to believe in the one-of-a-kind Son of God when introduced to him.

John 3:16-18 (The Message)

And then he told them, 'Go into all the world and preach the Good News to everyone. Anyone who believes and is baptized will be saved. But anyone who refuses to believe will be condemned.'

Mark 16:15-16 (NLT)

"So now I hope you can see, Jamie, that baptism is an integral part of covenant relationship that must not be left out. It is no more important or less important than any other step in the covenant. In ancient covenants, all these steps were required, but in the New Covenant Jesus reduced the requirements to only two: faith and baptism. But just as leaving out any step in the ancient covenant was unacceptable, leaving out either of the two steps in the New Covenant is just as deadly. In fact, as the King told Nicodemus, in order to enter the kingdom of heaven, all must be born of water and the spirit. They need a heart change, but that's not all. The heart change produces the faith required to obey the command and example of water baptism. Although there are many Scriptures that say you must believe and then you will be saved, these Scriptures all assume that this belief will result in obedient submission to water baptism. Baptism is irrelevant and pointless without faith, but faith is incomplete without baptism."

"I see. Now I think I understand!"

Note: The steps of the covenant used in this section of "What Might Be" are from The Covenant *by Jim Garlow.*

Chapter 3: Satan's Strategy

"This is no afternoon athletic contest that we'll walk away from and forget about in a couple of hours. This is for keeps, a life-or-death fight to the finish against the Devil and all his angels"

(Ephesians 6:12, The Message).

Dad Was A Man of Integrity

Dad truly was a man of integrity. To him, integrity meant more than just doing the right thing when no one was looking. It also meant making sure that church leaders at the congregations he served were examples of integrity.

When I became an adult, Dad and I got closer and closer. I could always share anything with him and he could call me to talk anytime. The one thing I was sure of was that when our conversation was over I would feel better than before we started. Dad oozed with encouragement; it emanated from him no matter who he was talking to.

After I had been away from home for about twenty years, he also began to share things with me that he couldn't talk to anyone else about. This is one of my saddest memories of Dad. I will never forget the worry and concern in his voice that he had over a Christian man he knew who had sacrificed his witness for the kingdom by becoming a habitual liar. Have you ever heard it said of someone, "They'd lie when the truth sounds better"? This correctly described this individual.

What would Dad do? He did the only thing he could do as a Christian man of integrity: he spent a year documenting the lying habits of this man, and then he confronted him privately. It weighed heavily on Dad's heart, but he had no choice.

Love for truth sometimes means you must do the unpleasant by confronting the lie. Did it go well? It went all right. It wasn't fun. The man wasn't happy, but the evidence was overwhelming, and he couldn't deny it. What was at stake? The man's eternal soul. Liars go to hell: "But cowards, unbelievers, the corrupt, murderers, the immoral, those who practice witchcraft, idol worshipers, and all liars—their fate is in the fiery lake of burning sulfur. This is the second death" (Revelation 21:8, NLT).

Satan Wants to Distort Our View of Heaven

Our world is slowly deteriorating. Erosion, decay, rust, and a variety of other realities make this cursed world only a shadow of the real and wonderful world to come where there will be no thieves to steal or rust to destroy (Matthew 6:19). The eternal world to come will be free of all death, disease, and evil people, but it takes the eyes of faith to see it.

"Faith is the substance of things hoped for, the evidence of things not seen" (Hebrews 11:1, NKJV).

I like those descriptive words that help put a solid foundation under my picture of heaven: "substance" and "evidence of things not seen." The original earth had substance. God walked on it with Adam. Heaven—the place we were truly made for—also has substance. God and Adam had a relationship on the solid foundation of a perfect, curse-free world, a place of substance.

But Satan interrupted the cycle, causing man to sin, death to begin, and deterioration to ravage the planet. It's now only a shadow of what it was then, and things will only get worse until the time for the final restoration of all things (Acts 3:21). In the interim before Jesus's return, it's been easy for us to get confused about what's valuable and what's not. This world—in its current state—does not have the same value as the world to come, the eternal heaven. I once heard a funny story that helps illustrate how distorted our perspective of heaven has become.

A man was startled awake in the middle of the night. It was an angel waking him with some surprising news.

"I'm coming for you tomorrow night. Your time is up. But I got you an exception to the rule. You will be allowed to bring one suitcase with you."

The next day, the man sold every asset he owned and converted it to gold bricks, which he put in a suitcase beside his bed.

Sure enough, the following night the angel arrived on schedule, and the man grabbed the suitcase as they flew away.

When they arrived at the pearly gates of heaven, the escorting angel dropped him off and flew away. The angel guardian of the gate looked up the man's name from a list of approved guests and found it. "Yes, here you are. Please come right in. But leave the suitcase behind; no earthly possessions are allowed inside."

At this, the man was frantic. "You don't understand. I was told they made an exception in my case and that I would be allowed to bring this one bag."

The angel, scratching his head in confusion, said he would have to contact St. Peter to make sure that was approved and then added, "Can I just see what's in the case?"

"Sure," said the man as he opened it for the angel to see.

The shocked and dismayed angel examined the contents and looked back up at the man. "Pavement? You brought pavement?"

Our most valuable possessions here are nothing to compare with the beauty and wonder of eternity, but Satan works hard to distort that truth.

Satan Works to Confuse

Satan is actively at work trying to confuse us on all kinds of important subjects, but I believe that he is especially focused on confusing us about heaven and hell, and that's why I feel such a compelling need to write this book about heaven. 2 Corinthians 4:3-4 reveals an important satanic strategy: Satan—the god of this world—has blinded our minds to the truth.

If you were Satan and you were trying to hurt God by taking as many people to hell with you as possible, wouldn't you try to confuse people about the true nature of heaven and hell? I would. Many books and movie situations work to portray heaven as boring and unattainable and hell as the place where all the fun activities will be. These tactics have been quite successful, even among Christians.

What is the most dominant view about what heaven will be like? "We'll be see-through people, sitting on the clouds, playing a harp, and worshiping God all day every day." Surprisingly, this is commonly accepted.

That doesn't even appeal to Christians, much less non-Christians. Personally, I think it's hogwash. Nobody wants a heaven that's like that. The prevailing response of the world to that idea is, "Let me just go to hell where all my friends will be; it sounds like a lot more fun than heaven. Besides, I'm not good enough to go to heaven anyway!"

Sad, isn't it? Sad that Christians have ignored the biblical realities of a wonderful, exciting eternity with endless exploration, unspeakable joy, and unending fun and fellowship, only to reduce it to something so dull and boring. Is God ever dull and boring? Or is it more accurate to describe his nature as intricately creative, infinitely thoughtful, and immaculately caring for his beloved children?

Satan's Deception of Homosexuality

I have been pretty vocal about my Christianity at the office. Years ago, one employee worked up the courage to approach me with a very sensitive topic. As he came into my office for a little talk, he shut my door. "I know this will get me fired," he said, "but I have to tell you something. I am a homosexual."

I knew he used to be active in a Baptist church, so I suspected he was struggling against this temptation. I think I surprised him with my answer, but I believe it helped him see the heart of God. I pray it did. I said, "I want you to know that God loves people who think they are homosexual, but he hates the practice of homosexuality. I pray that you become a tool of God to reach other people who think they are homosexual and bring them out of that lifestyle, out of that deception, and back to God. I pray you'll use this to help others get to heaven."

He was stunned. And he still had a job. Later, he did help other homosexuals. But I told him the truth in a loving way. At some point, we must love people enough to teach them the things that can steal eternal life from them—even if it hurts. Jesus came full of grace and truth: "The Word became flesh and made his dwelling among us. We have seen his glory, the glory of the One and Only, who came from the Father, full of grace and truth" (John 1:14, NIV).

Grace without truth leaves out details that may offend someone in order to avoid conflict or confrontation. But the omission of truth fails to lead them to eternal life; therefore, it isn't truly grace. Truth without grace is so legalistic and unfeeling that the sinner can't see the loving arms of the Savior past the cold-hearted facts—words like "you're headed to hell"—we often recite like a vending machine dispenses candy. Facts alone omit grace, and omitting grace causes others to see only a factual side of a Savior who died for them. These two—grace and truth—must go hand in hand in our lives just as they did in the life of Christ.

Notice how Jesus responded when he was confronted with the woman caught in the act of adultery: "Jesus stood up again and said to the woman, 'Where are your accusers? Didn't even one of them condemn you?' 'No, Lord,' she said. And Jesus said, 'Neither do I. Go and sin no more.'" (John 8:10-11, NLT).

He called her sin a sin, but he also offered her the grace of forgiveness even though she hadn't asked for it yet. Unforgiveness is an important satanic tool that easily entraps even the strongest Christians. How? Unforgiveness leads to self-centered, pride-filled bitterness.

Probably the best book I ever read that teaches this valuable lesson is *The Shack* by William P. Young. I recommend it strongly to anyone who struggles with forgiveness. If a name comes to mind as you consider this, focus on forgiving them and praying for them right now. That's the Holy Spirit convicting your heart. Don't ignore it. Act on it.

Love them enough to tell them the truth, but offer the truth with a kind heart, one that bleeds with obvious care for the person—just like Jesus.

It's a Spiritual Battle for the Mind

"The seed that fell on the hard path represents those who hear the message, but then the Devil comes and steals it away and prevents them from believing and being saved" (Luke 8:12, NLT).

The battle is for the human mind. Satan's weapon is to confuse people about truth and to discredit the Scriptures in every way possible. Luke 9:43-46 says that the disciples didn't know what Jesus was talking about when he said he was going to be betrayed.

The battle is in your mental faculties. Satan wants to hide the truth from you and keep you from clearly understanding the things going on around you and the things the Holy Spirit is teaching you through Scripture, godly friends, and circumstances. John 8:31-32 states that knowing the truth sets us free.

The battle is for truth, and it requires ongoing obedience. Obedience coupled with truth frees you from Satan's power. Romans 7:21-23 reveals that Paul even struggled with making the right decisions each day and that it took constant effort to fight his internal, sinful nature.

The battle is in your daily decisions. Relative to the subject of heaven, it's over what you believe about heaven. Satan wants you to believe what some men have taught—heaven is ethereal, only spiritual, with boring agendas, continual dull worship, and see-through, ghost-like bodies. Please keep in mind that there will be wonderful times of worship, but it definitely won't be dull or boring. It's in Satan's best interest to confuse you and lie to you about heaven and eternity—often propagating these lies through well-meaning religious teachers, preachers, and leaders. It's important to your present that you correctly interpret God's revelations about our heavenly future.

"No eye has seen, no ear has heard, no mind has conceived what God has prepared for those who love him" (1 Corinthians 2:9, NIV).

This passage is often used to teach that we can't know anything about heaven right now, but that's not true. Verses 10-12 reveal that since we have God's Spirit, we will be able to know much about heaven and eternity. This theme is repeated in 1 Corinthians 2:14-16 and 2 Corinthians 10:3-4.

Ephesians 6:10-18 teaches us that Satan has all kinds of strategies and tricks. But according to Revelation 13:6, the heart of his strategy is a deception about heaven. According to this passage, the successful antidote for us against this contagious virus is to pray about it. Try praying for your mind and heart to be opened to see the truth about your eternal home.

Satan rebelled against God. When he did, he lost his powerful position of authority that apparently placed him above all the rest of the angelic host. As Revelation 13:6 reveals, he now slanders heaven. If he can't steal our inheritance from us, he then shifts his focus to slander the King and the King's home, heaven. If he can convince us that heaven isn't indescribably beautiful and wonderful, then his goal of permanently changing our eternal destination—to hell instead of heaven—is much easier to accomplish. In my personal opinion, he's done a masterful job. If Christians aren't excited about heaven, then Christians won't be excited about taking others there with them. Evangelism will become extinct with this kind of thinking, and it almost has. Pray for a healthier view of heaven. Our evangelistic spirit is at stake.

Satan Wants Fear to Dominate Our Thoughts about the Future

Have you ever enjoyed a book so much that you reread it? I have. We all have different interests, and my favorite books are adventure stories. There are very few that have warranted repeating, but I think I enjoyed those few the second time even more than I did the first.

As I reread an adventure story recently, I found that I not only noticed interesting and exciting details the second time through that I'd missed the first time, but I also noticed that my enjoyment came from the journey more so than from the ending. Does that make sense? The second time through, I knew how it would end, and the joy of actually putting myself in the character and experiencing the storyline from that point of view was what brought the pleasure. In short, I enjoyed the moment, the experience, without a worry about the ending, because I knew it would come out all right.

I believe it's possible—even probable—that this is the view the Lord takes as he observes and interacts in the daily experiences of our life. He knows just how things are going to end and knows it will be all right, so the thrill comes from enjoying the experience and watching us grow and learn. Think through this with me and see if you don't agree: in your mind, in your thoughts, where do you spend most of your time? Do you focus on the past, the present, or the future?

Some are bitter about how they have been treated or about some sad, depressing event that has hurt them deeply in the past. Maybe they were abused, taken advantage of, cheated, or lied to. Perhaps they have experienced the devastating loss of the death of a child, a spouse, a close friend, or a mentor. Some live in that experience by making that ugly past a daily, minute-by-minute part of their present. Their thoughts constantly wander back to that sad, depressing event to the point of robbing them of their present.

Others let the future paralyze their present. They wake up at night imagining that all the things that could ruin their future are bound to happen, and they then lose even more sleep by working out plans of action for each bad scenario. Have you ever lay there at night going over all your worries and problems? Did you ever notice that the more you think about it all, the worse it gets? Satan does his best work in the dark. More often than not, the light of day makes those seemingly overwhelming circumstances vanish like fog on a sunny day. It almost never works out as badly as we imagined when we worried about it all night.

Imagination. Creativity. These are qualities that are a vital part of mankind's being created in the image—imagination—of God. Your imagination actually reveals how you're like the King, but Satan works to hijack that King-like quality by turning your imagination against you. Satan steals your assured, eternal, happy future from the present by distorting the reality of heaven and by making you focus your imagination on fear of what might happen instead of the glories of what might be. Worry is focusing on what you don't want to happen. Worry and fear cannot coexist with faith. One cancels out the other. Fear is really faith in Satan. Faith in God is, in reality, a rejection of the fear and worry that Satan wants you to focus on.

There is some benefit from glancing back at your past, and there are some ways you can learn from it and improve your life. But don't dwell on it. A disappointing past can throw a "wet blanket" on your present and take the joy out of the steps of progress you have made so far in overcoming it. Dwelling on a successful past can cause you to have an unhealthy, self-centered, cocky confidence in the present, making you think that God is so pleased with you that he would refuse to let anything bad happen to you. Ever. That wasn't true about Jesus. He did nothing wrong, and bad things happened to him.

I believe that there is great benefit in the realization that Satan has worked hard to stifle our imagination and creativity about our eternal future: heaven. Be encouraged to think and meditate on heaven. Hebrews 13:14 tells us to look forward to the city that's to come. Ephesians 1:18 records Paul's prayer for the believers: that our hearts will be flooded with understanding about our rich inheritance—heaven. And Philippians 3:19-21 reveals that we are already counted as citizens of heaven. We must eagerly look forward to the return of Jesus Christ.

Do You Trust God Totally?

If your religious background taught you to hold an opinion on a subject that conflicts with Scripture, what would you do? You have two choices: you can change your view to match the Scripture, or you can say, "This doesn't mean what it looks like it says; it really means something else." Once Satan got Christians to begin to doubt Genesis 1, it became easier to get Christians to doubt other teachings, ideas, and concepts throughout the Scriptures. Let me give you an example from a real event in my life.

I have a habit of getting up early and going to breakfast alone to do my Bible study and praying. When people see you reading a Bible in a public place like Burger King, they immediately assume you are a preacher. Only preachers read their Bibles, right?

One morning, a religious man came up to me as I was reading and began a conversation. He immediately directed the conversation to his opinion that his church group was the only group that worshiped God, all others made the mistake of worshiping Jesus. His main point was that "The Lord God is one God" and, therefore, Jesus could not be part of God, even though he certainly was a good man. In other words, he thought Jesus was a good man, but he wasn't God.

Next, he gave me a book written by a man who would give me a more complete understanding of the Bible. I asked why I needed something other than the Bible itself. He avoided the question. With him standing right there, I immediately turned to John 1: "In the beginning was the Word, and the Word was with God, and the Word was God. And the Word became flesh and dwelt among us, and we beheld His glory, the glory as of the only begotten of the Father, full of grace and truth" (John 1:1, 14, NKJV).

This passage just shattered his belief that Jesus was not God. Now he had to choose. Would he choose the man-made book, or would he choose the inspired Word of God? He chose the former. Did his choice change the truth? No.

You Have the Same Choice about Heaven

What will you do? If a closer study of the Bible reveals new insights about the spiritual realm and your eternal future, will you choose to think like you've always thought, or will you change your opinion to match the Scriptures? It's your choice. And although it's not technically a salvation issue, your attitude about it could drastically change your outlook about evangelism. If this new idea about eternity gets you as excited about the future as I think it will, you won't be able to stand not taking more people with you.

John teaches that the Holy Spirit leads us and guides us in our pursuit of truth: "There is so much more I want to tell you, but you can't bear it now. When the Spirit of truth comes, he will guide you into all truth. He will not speak on his own but will tell you what he has heard. He will tell you about the future" (John 16:12-13, NLT).

Although there are some unique exceptions in Scripture, Acts 2:38-40 teaches that normal procedure for receiving the Holy Spirit is by submitting to baptism. Once you become a Christian, the Holy Spirit is instrumental in guiding you to the truth of a matter by opening your eyes to greater and deeper levels of understanding (1 Corinthians 2:11-12). The Holy Spirit is a prerequisite to a fuller and more correct understanding about heaven.

Satan's Deception About Heaven

While Jesus presents himself as the Way, the Truth, and the Life (John 14:1), Satan's forces are at work as spirits of deception throughout the world (1 John 4:5-6). And what's a more important deception than twisting the truth about our goal—heaven and eternity with God? "For a time is coming when people will no longer listen to right teaching. They will follow their own desires and will look for teachers who will tell them whatever they want to hear. They will reject the truth and follow strange myths" (2 Timothy 4:3-4, NLT).

In many ways, this time is upon us. Strange myths abound about the planet, the future, the kingdom, and the truth: Jesus is the Redeemer of the people and the planet.

God Has Power Greater Than Satan's Destruction

Satan would love for us to believe that his power to destroy God's good and perfect creation is greater than God's power to create it or restore it. But Scripture teaches otherwise: "God alone, who gave the law, is the Judge. He alone has the power to save or to destroy" (James 4:12, NLT). At present, it may appear that Satan has been successful at destroying creation by leading mankind into rebellion against God, which led to all death, disease, and the curse on the earth, but this verse from James reveals that isn't true.

First of all, note that God put the curse on the planet. Genesis 8:21 says that God cursed the earth; he spoke the curse into reality, just as he spoke the world into reality. The curse is the reason for pain, thorns, decay, death, disease, rust, and everything else that destroys.

Secondly, and probably more importantly, Acts 3 reveals that our world won't ultimately stay in its current state. If it did, wouldn't this in itself be an admission that Satan's power to destroy is greater than God's power to create—or recreate—since Satan's rebellion led us all down this path? No, things won't stay like this. God has great plans for restoration and resurrection, showing that his power of recreation is greater than Satan's power to destroy.

Satan Wants Us to Overlook These Verses on Heaven

2 Corinthians 4:18, Philippians 3:19-20, and Colossians 3:1-2 all offer encouragement for us to focus our lives and thoughts on heaven instead of the things of this world. Hebrews 11:13-16 adds that those in the faith hall of fame were all focused on the glories and wonders of the next world instead of the current one because this one isn't our permanent one.

Satan Uses Misdirection, Deception, and Scriptural Misapplication

There was an old joke Dad used to love that helps illustrate how Satan tries to get us to misapply scriptural truth. It goes like this:

A friend came over and asked, "Can I borrow your new ladder?"

"No," I said. "I'm going fishing on Tuesday."

"What does going fishing on Tuesday have to do with my borrowing your ladder?" the friend asked.

"Nothing. But if I don't want you to borrow my ladder, one excuse is as good as another."

Actually, Satan is better at it than that illustration, but the translation of some passages from the original Greek into English can lead to false assumptions. The Greek was a perfect language to preserve the original text, because it is so much more descriptive than English. Let's talk about the word "love," for example.

In English, we "love" pizza, we "love" adventure, or we "love" our spouses. The same word—love—has three very different meanings. The first one applies to our physical taste buds, the second to the emotional excitement often experienced when we see an adventure film or read a great story, and the third applies to a special, one-person centered, lifetime relationship. But in the Greek, these realities are communicated by three completely different Greek words.

Similarly, there are some Bible passages that on the surface seem to discredit the idea of a literal, physical, eternal kingdom, and these need to be dealt with individually, giving the proper consideration to the original Greek, the surrounding context, and how they must integrate into the long list of passages that seem to point in a completely different direction. Ultimately, since all Scripture is profitable for training us (2 Timothy 3:16), so if there is an apparent conflict by a short list of passages, we must dig a little deeper to see if they truly contradict or not.

But Jesus Said His Kingdom Was Not of This World

One of the best examples of this is seen when some point to the statement by Jesus saying that his kingdom was not of this world. "Jesus said, 'My kingdom is not of this world. If it were, my servants would fight to prevent my arrest by the Jews. But now my kingdom is from another place'" (John 18:36, NIV).

Actually, the verse itself is enough commentary since it explains itself in the last sentence. Jesus doesn't say that his kingdom isn't "in" this world or "for" this world, it's not "from" here, it's from another place. The Bible Knowledge Commentary puts it this way, "It is not of this world; it is from another place, that is, heaven. Therefore it comes not by rebellion but by submission to God." Wiersbe's Expository Outlines says, "His kingdom is of a spiritual nature, within people's hearts. One day when He returns, He will establish His kingdom on earth." And the Jamieson, Fausset, and Brown Commentary states, "He does not say it is not 'in' or 'over,' but it is not 'of this world,' that is, in its origin and nature."

But Jesus Said the Earth Would Disappear

"Heaven and earth will disappear, but my words will remain forever" (Matthew 24:35, NLT).

Although at first glance this verse appears to contradict all the other verses that have been indicating a "heaven on earth" possibility, but if this verse is actually saying earth will be annihilated, then it also means heaven will be annihilated too. Obviously, this is not the case.

Note that the Greek word used here for "earth" is literally the soil, but the Greek here for "heaven" means the abode of God. The answer may lie in an understanding that God destroyed the earth with a flood, but the earth is still here. In 2 Peter 3:7 God reveals his plan for earth: destruction by fire. But like the first destruction by flood, this will be a purification of the planet instead of an annihilation. Everything evil, impure, unclean, painful, or destructive will be burned up, leaving only good things, good deeds done for the right reasons (1 Corinthians 3:12-15), and good people.

Jesus Said Some of the Disciples Would See the Kingdom Come

"I assure you that some of you standing here right now will not die before you see me, the Son of Man, coming in my kingdom" (Matthew 16:28, NLT).

It's not insignificant to note here that the Greek word translated "some" is "tis," which actually means "a person, a body, or a man." So Jesus specifically said some of those standing there would not die before seeing him come in his kingdom. All the disciples who heard Jesus make this statement were still alive a few days later at Pentecost, so why didn't he just say, "*All* of you will live to see me coming in my kingdom"? Although the events of that Pentecost did usher in the beginning of the church—the first phase of the kingdom—he must be talking about something else; probably the actual beginning of eternity: heaven, the permanent, ultimate kingdom. He meant the second coming.

Although everyone may not accept this idea, I ask you to consider this possibility: John wrote down his vision of the Son of Man coming in his kingdom. It's called the book of Revelation, the final book in the Bible. He saw it all in a vision. Also, keep in mind that throughout Scripture, the predominant theme that is repeated over and over is the idea of the second "coming" and the "coming" of the kingdom. These are the words God chose. He could have just as easily talked about "the great exodus" or "the great departure" to the kingdom, but he didn't. I believe he used the right words.

Daniel 10, Interface Between Seen and Unseen

Daniel 10 is one of the most insightful passages in Scripture, giving us a glimpse into the unseen. Daniel had been praying for three weeks when an angel shows up as an answer to his prayer: "Don't be afraid, Daniel. Since the first day you began to pray for understanding and to humble yourself before your God, your request has been heard in heaven. I have come in answer to your prayer. But for twenty-one days the spirit prince of the kingdom of Persia blocked my way. Then Michael, one of the archangels, came to help me, and I left him there with the spirit prince of the kingdom of Persia" (Daniel 10:12-13, NLT).

A few verses later, the angel mentions this battle again: "Soon I must return to fight against the spirit prince of the kingdom of Persia, and after that the spirit prince of the kingdom of Greece will come" (Daniel 10:20-21, NLT).

What was happening in the unseen? When Daniel began to pray, an angel was dispatched to bring an answer, but a spirit prince from the kingdom of Persia fought to prevent that answer from coming. This fight had lasted for three weeks, and the entire time Daniel was continuing to pray for that answer. Then the angel got help. Michael, an archangel, showed up and took the place of the angel. This freed him to bring the answer. However, the battle was not over—far from it. And not only did this angel possess the knowledge that he was to return and continue the fight against the spirit prince from that kingdom of Persia, he was also fully aware that the next great battle was to be against the spirit prince of the kingdom of Greece. Do you remember from your history classes the world kingdom that followed the Medo-Persian Empire? It was the Greek kingdom, led by Alexander the Great.

Translation? In the unseen, there are rulers, powers, and authorities who are designated to protect and defend certain territories. Territorial angels, territorial demons, just as it is stated in Ephesians 6 and many other places: "We are not fighting against flesh-and-blood enemies, but against evil rulers and authorities of the unseen world, against mighty powers in this dark world, and against evil spirits in the heavenly places" (Ephesians 6:12, NLT).

Many Demons Are Named in Scripture

After I began noticing all these passages in Scripture about how our true enemy is unseen and how there are principalities, powers, and evil spirits in a world unseen by human eyes, my new awareness of the subject opened my eyes to notice many other demonic entities listed by name throughout the Bible.

I admit that this whole idea was a little unnerving at first, but as I began to accept this possibility—now a reality—I also began to notice that every time a Bible verse mentioned the name of a demonic entity, the territory that entity was in charge of—or assigned to—was also listed. This made it even more real to me. In some unspoken way, it began to dawn on me that there are actually demons—fallen angels—who serve the purposes of Satan by working to encourage the same rebellion in us that Satan had encouraged in them. Slowly but surely, a whole new world of understanding began to unfold in my daily Bible study that I had never known before.

2 Kings 17:29-31 unveils several demonic entities by name. Succoth-benith was god of Babylon; Nergal was over the city of Cuthah; Ashima was over the Samarian city of Hamath. In addition, Nibhas and Tartak were assigned to the region of the Avvites, and Adrammelech and Anammelech were gods in the area of Sepharvaim. Now add the revelation from 1 Corinthians 10:20 that states that sacrifices offered to these entities were actually being offered to demons, and you start to get the true picture of the spiritual war at work in the unseen.

When I finally put all this together in my mind, the unseen reality looked something like this: When God created the world, he set up principalities, authorities, and powers in the unseen world. When Satan led his rebellion against God, some of these followed him, turning their backs on God and the faithful host of heaven. In fact, angels are often called "the starry host"—note the meaning of the Hebrew word in verses like Isaiah 40:26—so some commentaries believe that Revelation 12:4 reveals that about one third of the angelic host followed Satan's rebellion against God.

Since we also know that Satan prowls around the earth like a roaring lion looking for someone to devour (1 Peter 5:8), it makes sense that he's getting reports from his evil, demonic forces about their progress in leading other humans away from God in every possible way. Couple this with the reality that all demons in Scripture have an assigned territory, and you unveil a hierarchy—a rank and file of evil forces—working against whatever God is promoting. This includes the great, wonderful, and beautifully perfect unseen reality—heaven. One of Satan's main goals is to dispel the notion that heaven is worth more than everything you've got. He's doing everything he possibly can to tarnish the luster of heaven and enhance the lies about hell.

In this, he's actually been quite successful. I have heard it said repeatedly over the years, "I'm not good enough for heaven, but I'd rather be in hell with all my friends, anyway." Nobody is good enough for heaven, but Christ is. Put on Christ in obedient, believers' baptism, and that clothing alone has the power to gain you entrance.

Jesus Confirms Satan's Kingdom

Notice how Jesus responds to Satan's temptation: "The devil took him to the peak of a very high mountain and showed him the kingdoms of the world and all their glory. 'I will give it all to you,' he said, 'if you will kneel down and worship me.' 'Get out of here, Satan,' Jesus told him. 'For the Scriptures say, 'You must worship the LORD your God and serve only him'" (Matthew 4:8-10, NLT).

The most significant observation about this situation may be what Jesus did not say. He didn't say, "Satan, you can't offer me what isn't yours," or "These kingdoms of the world are already mine." Why? Because as Scripture confirms, those kingdoms were Satan's to offer: "Satan, who is the god of this world, has blinded the minds of those who don't believe" (2 Corinthians 4:4, NLT).

When did Satan gain that position? When Adam and Eve sinned in the Garden of Eden. That's when Adam gave up his God-given authority. It's sad, but it's true.

But Didn't Jesus Say He Had All Authority?

Yes, he did: "Jesus came to them and said, 'All authority in heaven and on earth has been given to me'" (Matthew 28:18, NIV).

Then how does this dovetail into the passages calling Satan the "prince of the power of the air" and the "god of this world"? It fits by adding one small but important detail about the ultimate, complete authority of Jesus over all things everywhere. Hebrews reveals that this is a future reality rather than a current one. It's what I call the "not yet" property: "Now in putting everything in subjection to him, he left nothing outside his control. At present, we do not yet see everything in subjection to him" (Hebrews 2:8, ESV).

The Final Blow to Satan's Authority

The final nail in Satan's coffin of authority is revealed in 1 Corinthians, where it states not only that Christ will return to destroy death planet-wide, but also that he will remove Satan as the planet's ruler and authority and claim it for his own. Note the wording of the passage is such that we learn that earth is the kingdom: "The end will come, when he will turn the kingdom over to God the Father, having destroyed every ruler and authority and power. For Christ must reign until he humbles all his enemies beneath his feet. And the last enemy to be destroyed is death" (1 Corinthians 15:24-26, NLT).

The simple statement that the kingdom will be turned over to God indicates that the world is the kingdom. It's the only area temporarily outside the authority of the Godhead, as the verses about Christ that were just covered show.

The Kingdom Comes in at Least Two Phases

Jesus himself shows repeatedly (Matthew 12:28, Mark 7:29, Acts 10:38, etc.) that the removal of demons, sickness, and evil spirits of every kind characterize the kingdom's coming:

This is not to say that the church isn't the doorway into the kingdom that many have supposed. On the contrary, the church is the mechanism chosen by the King to usher in the beginning phase of the kingdom: "He asked them, 'But who do you say I am?' Simon Peter answered, 'You are the Messiah, the Son of the living God.' Jesus replied, 'You are blessed, Simon son of John, because my Father in heaven has revealed this to you. You did not learn this from any human being. Now I say to you that you are Peter [which means 'rock'], and upon this rock I will build my church, and all the powers of hell will not conquer it'" (Matthew 16:15-18, NLT).

As this confirms, the church is the usher that ultimately will escort the King to earth at the second coming. Permanently. Revelation 21:3-4 reveals the ultimate plan of God: to come live with us, wipe our tears, and remove pain and death forever.

This is the future reality that Satan wants you confused about. Here is the truth: a future, perfect, sinless planet where everyone is good, kind, and loving is a world we can really get excited about. It's a world that we can become so excited about that we want others to join us in it. In other words, a biblical understanding of a real world with love, fellowship, unending joy, and relationship with the One you were created for is a world that inspires evangelism in the present, death-filled, sin-sick world. It's definitely in Satan's best interest to squelch the true nature of that future reality; that way he keeps more of us from becoming residents there. I vote we change that. How about you?

Summary

In summary, all these passages on spiritual warfare reveal Satan's war with God and that his strategy includes distorting the truth about heaven in every possible way.

What Might Be: The True Location of the Kingdom

"Okay, Jamie, today's lesson begins from the book of Matthew in the new covenant."

"The new covenant?"

"Yes. Messiah was predicted through the Old Testament to bring a new covenant, and that's just what Jesus did. Forgive me, I often forget that most from your time period called it the New Testament."

"Oh, okay. Yes, the New Testament. Matthew?"

"Yes, Matthew 13:36-43. 'Then, leaving the crowds outside, Jesus went into the house. His disciples said, "Please explain to us the story of the weeds in the field." Jesus replied, "The Son of Man is the farmer who plants the good seed. The field is the world, and the good seed represents the people of the kingdom. The weeds are the people who belong to the evil one. The enemy who planted the weeds among the wheat is the devil. The harvest is the end of the world, and the harvesters are the angels. Just as the weeds are sorted out and burned in the fire, so it will be at the end of the world. The Son of Man will send his angels, and they will remove from his kingdom everything that causes sin and all who do evil. And the angels will throw them into the fiery furnace, where there will be weeping and gnashing of teeth. Then the righteous will shine like the sun in their Father's kingdom. Anyone with ears to hear should listen and understand!'

"Jamie, although you did not quite understand the connection between your physical world and eternity, these words from the lips of the King are perhaps the best ones to help you understand. Before I explain the passage, you would be best served by knowing some scientific background of experts from your time. A little known fact—especially to Christians—is the scientific support for the biblical position of unseen worlds. Many from your time period and geography believed that all those in the unseen—like the angelic host—were ethereal in nature."

"Ethereal? What does that mean?"

"Ghostly, see-through, without substance, or only spiritual in nature as opposed to a form with solid attributes. This in spite of Jesus' assertion to his disciples to touch his side and feel his hands. This was recorded in the guidebook in an effort to squelch what the King knew in advance would be a problem for many. Note that he also ate and drank with them to add emphasis to that fact. His resurrection body was real, tangible, solid.

"In truth—as scientists from your twentieth century discovered—there are multiple realities. Experts from your time, for example, discovered that there are at least ten dimensions, a fact we knew from the beginning. Each of these is just as solid as your world but completely invisible to your eyes. The best way to categorize these is the term 'alternate realities.'

"Jacob's dream was a good analogy to help you relate to this fact: Genesis 28:12-13 states, 'He [Jacob] dreamed, and behold, a ladder was set up on the earth, and its top reached to heaven; and there the angels of God were ascending and descending on it. And behold, the LORD stood above it and said: "I am the LORD God of Abraham your father and the God of Isaac; the land on which you lie I will give to you and your descendants."'

"Just as Solomon's request for wisdom came through a dream, Jacob dreamed of the unseen world where we abide. In Jacob's dream, the King offered a simple picture of the true reality: the entire unseen realm where we live is simply out of sight, hidden. It is solid, permanent, and tangible, just invisible to you—for now. In the dream, there is a ladder and a stairway that connects our world with yours. When yours is transformed to become permanent, what really happens is that our world will invade yours, our reality transforms yours, merging them into one. Then your restored world will again be part of our reality. The two will combine permanently.

"Now let us apply this to the passage for today. Jesus used stories to illustrate eternal realities. In this parable from Matthew, the King dispels the notion that the saved are gathered and removed to some unearthly place. Notice that the King arrives with the angelic host and sends them out to all parts of the earth—near and far—to remove from the kingdom all evil people and everything that causes mankind to sin. In other words, he cleans up the kingdom. These evil ones are thrown out of the kingdom, into a fiery place far away from earth. This will allow the godly—still present in the kingdom—to shine in his glory and serve the King face to face.

"The rebel creature—Satan—has worked hard to discredit or change this simple message. And he has been quite successful in certain parts of the world. But deception concerning a biblical reality does not change the true nature of that reality."

"Wow. That's so different from what I had pictured. But it makes sense now, and the simplicity of it makes it all the more profound."

Chapter 4: Purification by Fire

They conveniently forget that long ago all the galaxies
and this very planet were brought into existence out of
watery chaos by God's word. Then God's word brought
the chaos back in a flood that destroyed the world. The
current galaxies and earth are fuel for the final fire. God
is poised, ready to speak his word again, ready to give
the signal for the judgment and destruction of the des-
ecrating skeptics.

2 Peter 3:5-7 (The Message)

I heard the count and saw both horses and riders in
my vision: fiery breastplates on the riders, lion heads on
the horses breathing out fire and smoke and brimstone.
With these three weapons—fire and smoke and brimstone—they killed a third of the human race.

Revelation 9:16-18 (The Message)

Dad's Attitude Toward Others

In a gentle, special way, small-town people realize their need for
everyone else. People are just friendlier. Dad waved at every car
we met on the highway. He never tired of doing it. There weren't
very many cars—not in a town of two thousand. I think that all
people in small towns are friendlier than those in big cities, but
I might think that way because Dad thought like that.

One day, Mom's curiosity found voice. "Why do you wave at
every car we pass? Most of them never wave back."

Dad said, "Oh, if they had seen me in time, they would have waved. They probably waved back just after we passed."

That's how Dad thought. He always thought the best about people. He believed they were good, even when they acted otherwise. And then when they'd proved him wrong, he'd often defend them saying, "Someone must have been unkind to them in the past for them to act that way. They just need to be taught what's right, and they'll change." Looking back on Dad's unwavering attitude of encouragement toward others, I think he truly had the heart of the Savior and the ability to look at people through the eyes of Jesus.

Compassion and kindness marked the life of my Dad, just like it did the life of Jesus. But compassion didn't keep Jesus from describing a place of eternal torment for those who didn't accept him: "The rich man also died and was buried. In hell, where he was in torment, he looked up and saw Abraham far away, with Lazarus by his side" (Luke 16:22-23, NIV).

Fire and brimstone is an old style of preaching that isn't practiced much anymore in spite of the scriptural warning: "The fear of the LORD is the beginning of wisdom" (Psalm 111:10, ESV).

Fear the Fire of the Coming Wrath of God

As I went through my Bible and highlighted every verse in yellow that gave any possible hint about heaven and our eternal existence, several unexpected patterns emerged, not the least of which was the purification fires from God that will be designed to purge the planet of all evil and evil people. Sure, I knew that hints of this theme existed in connection with judgment or eternal punishment, but as I began looking closer at the specific details the verses offered, that's not exactly how this common thread in Scripture emerged. Let me explain.

It's easy to associate fire with hell, since everyone has read or heard the verses that link the two. This was much more subtle.

At least it was as the idea first emerged into my consciousness. The first passage that explained this theme that was growing in my mind like a budding rose was 1 Peter 1:7, which describes how our faith is being made more valuable to God by being tested by trials, like gold is purified by the heat of the refiner's fire.

Then I made the mental connection between judgment and fire as it relates to salvation that's described in 1 Corinthians:

> On the judgment day, fire will reveal what kind of work each builder has done. The fire will show if a person's work has any value. If the work survives, that builder will receive a reward. But if the work is burned up, the builder will suffer great loss. The builder will be saved, but like someone barely escaping through a wall of flames.
>
> 1 Corinthians 3:13-15 (NLT)

This really caught my eye, since it described people who are actually saved but lost many potential rewards due to some flaw in the person or in the person's motivation for doing good things for the kingdom. Sure, they made it to eternal life, but not with the vast rewards they could have had. It seemed like a paradox at first, like getting into heaven but being disappointed because of losing your suitcase along the way—the suitcase you were promised you could bring with you.

Then I made the final connection that seemed to make sense out of this confusion. It was like working out the solution to a small, metal toy puzzle I used to play with as a kid. It was made from two horseshoes with the ends welded to short chains that connected them together. A small metal ring—not big enough to slip over the horseshoe—was encircling the chain that connected the horseshoes together. You had to twist the horseshoes together just right to enable the ring to slip off and be separated. Once you learned the delicate maneuver, you could dazzle your friends after they declared it impossible. Once it clicked, the answer became obvious and the maneuver was repeatable. One day, the various passages that confirmed my theory clicked, and it all began to make perfect sense, scripturally speaking. Here's what I mean.

You can do many good things for the kingdom of God that would normally bring great rewards but don't result in the expected reward because you did them for wrong, selfish reasons. You could give money to a good cause so you can brag about it later. You can volunteer in a soup kitchen because it would help your business when you tell others about your involvement. You could sponsor a charitable event just to gain respect or admiration. There are any number of possibilities. In short, you can do the right thing for the wrong reasons. And if you do, it does you no good. It doesn't keep you from heaven, but you lose the tremendous blessing of potential, eternal rewards because you had the wrong motive for doing the right thing. 1 Chronicles 28:9, Proverbs 20:27, Luke 5:22, Acts 1:24, and Hebrews 4:13 all indicate that God knows the exact motives for everything we do.

Finally, this theme was confirmed to me by the instruction to be generous givers. We are told to give, but to not even let our left hand know what our right hand is doing: "When you give to someone in need, don't let your left hand know what your right hand is doing. Give your gifts in private, and your Father, who sees everything, will reward you" (Matthew 6:3-4, NLT).

So when we reject this advice and do good things to be seen, we just lost the reward for that good deed. Salvation is a gift, but rewards are earned. Let's not confuse the two. With that as the backdrop, I offer the following verses that give credence to the scriptural theme of purification by fire.

Purification by Fire: Old Testament Support

The first appearance of fire in Scripture comes as a direct result of sin in Eden. Angels used flaming swords to keep mankind separated from the tree of life.

> So the LORD God banished them from the Garden of Eden, and he sent Adam out to cultivate the ground from which he had been made. After sending them out, the LORD God stationed mighty cherubim to the east of the Garden of Eden. And he placed a flaming sword that flashed back and forth to guard the way to the tree of life.
>
> Genesis 3:23-24 (NLT)

Apparently a Holy God can walk freely with Adam before the first sin, but he can't come into direct contact with a sin-cursed planet. How different things were at this point from how they were in the sin-free garden of Eden.

"All Mount Sinai was covered with smoke because the LORD had descended on it in the form of fire. The smoke billowed into the sky like smoke from a furnace, and the whole mountain shook with a violent earthquake" (Exodus 19:18, NLT).

Deuteronomy expands on this theme a little further: "The LORD came from Mount Sinai and dawned upon us from Mount Seir; he shone forth from Mount Paran and came from Meribah-kadesh with flaming fire at his right hand" (Deuteronomy 33:2, NLT).

Elijah was one of only two people in Scripture who went to be with God without dying. Elijah's mode of transportation is recorded in 2 Kings 2:11-17: heavenly horses and chariots of fire. And just like Mt. Sinai, we see fire involved as the holy comes in contact with the sin-cursed earth, confirming that things from a holy reality cannot touch things on a sin-stained earth without the insulation of other-worldly purification fires.

At the dedication of the temple, we see another example of fire coming from the LORD's presence as he contacts our realm, and although God was not in physical form, the temple was occupied by him in such a way that the priests could not enter. What would it have been like to have witnessed the fire, smoke, and cloud of God that entered and filled his temple? I imagine those who witnessed this event talked about it for the rest of their lives.

"When Solomon finished praying, fire flashed down from heaven and burned up the burnt offerings and sacrifices, and the glorious presence of the LORD filled the Temple. The priests could not even enter the Temple of the LORD because the glorious presence of the LORD filled it" (2 Chronicles 7:1-2, NLT).

This verse from Psalm 18 isn't the only scriptural reference to a passageway connecting the seen realm to the unseen. Revelation 4:1 is one of the other places that mentions the existence of a door that currently shuts us off from the dimension of eternity. It reveals the fiery presence of the King as he enters our world and takes command of his entire creation. This will be quite a sight to witness some day.

> He opened the heavens and came down; dark storm clouds were beneath his feet. Mounted on a mighty angel, he flew, soaring on the wings of the wind. He shrouded himself in darkness, veiling his approach with dense rain clouds. The brilliance of his presence broke through the clouds, raining down hail and burning coals. The LORD thundered from heaven; the Most High gave a mighty shout. He shot his arrows and scattered his enemies; his lightning flashed, and they were greatly confused. Then at your command, O LORD, at the blast of your breath, the bottom of the sea could be seen, and the foundations of the earth were laid bare.

> Psalm 18:9-15 (NLT)

This next verse could be included in a list called "Old Testament Beatitudes." No doubt is left about who disappears and who remains in the land. In these three short verses, it is twice stated that the good people will get the land. Good doesn't always win over evil in the world as we know it, but God has plans for a future world where only good people are left in the land.

> For the wicked will be destroyed, but those who trust in the Lord will possess the land. In a little while, the wicked will disappear. Though you look for them, they will be gone. Those who are gentle and lowly will possess the land; they will live in prosperous security.
>
> Psalm 37:9-11 (nlt)

Earth has godly people and wicked people. The wicked will someday disappear. Will you still be here? Also notice the smoke analogy connected to the disappearance of the evil people. Where there's smoke, there's fire. "But the wicked will perish. The Lords' enemies are like flowers in a field—they will disappear like smoke" (Psalm 37:20, nlt).

It may appear that God's promises about the land and its cleansing from wickedness are myth because of how long ago he made them, but don't lose your patience. He will act. He will honor the godly. He will give you the land. And you will witness the destruction and removal of the wicked! God's promises are always true. "Don't be impatient for the Lord to act! Travel steadily along his path. He will honor you, giving you the land. You will see the wicked destroyed" (Psalm 37:34, nlt).

Here we have another passage with earth-melting fire from God: "The nations are in an uproar, and kingdoms crumble! God thunders, and the earth melts!" (Psalm 46:6, nlt).

The following passage appears to be a revelation of God's approaching earth to cleanse it with his holy fire, place his throne on Mt. Zion in Jerusalem, and summon all humanity to stand before him. Note that east and west are physical, earthly terms that would not likely apply to a surreal, floating, ghost-like existence.

> The mighty God, the Lord, has spoken; he has summoned all humanity from east to west! From Mount Zion, the perfection of beauty, God shines in glorious radiance. Our God approaches with the noise of thunder. Fire devours everything in his way, and a great storm rages around him.
>
> Psalm 50:1-3 (NLT)

Again, in the context of wicked people, this says that God will remove them and then avenge injustice. But the kicker for those who believe earth has no future is the last part of verse 11: God will reward goodness, and he will judge justly "here on earth." Since we know this is not the current state of affairs, it follows that this has a future fulfillment here on earth. Those who refuse to accept this possibility are left with spiritualizing or allegorizing this and every other passage that leads to this conclusion. If the allegorical position is taken, there is nothing to keep one from spiritualizing or allegorizing many other things: heaven, baptism, the resurrection, and even salvation. If you took that position, where would it stop? As can readily be seen in society today, it doesn't stop. Even the beautiful truths about Jesus Christ like the virgin birth and the resurrection have been emasculated by being called "symbolic" or "interesting" by many in the world, but certainly not "real" and especially not "literal." Be careful what you assign to allegory.

> "God will sweep them away, both young and old, faster than a pot heats on an open flame. The godly will rejoice when they see injustice avenged. They will wash their feet in the blood of the wicked. Then at last everyone will say, 'There truly is a reward for those who live for

God; surely there is a God who judges justly here on earth.' "

Psalm 58:9-11 (NLT)

When God appears, the wicked will die. This also implies that the godly will live. "Arise, O God, and scatter your enemies. Let those who hate God run for their lives. Drive them off like smoke blown by the wind. Melt them like wax in fire. Let the wicked perish in the presence of God" (Psalm 68:1-2, NLT).

The fire of God consumes his enemies, but does not harm his own. "Fire goes forth before him and burns up all his foes" (Psalm 97:3, NLT). Note that it is common throughout prophetic scripture for a future event to be referred to in the past tense. An example of this is seen in how Isaiah referred to Jesus when he said, "He was led as a lamb to slaughter," and "He opened not his mouth." In this next passage—just as the LORD came in fire as hot as a fiery furnace when he descended from his cloud-throne onto Sinai—God will repeat this type of event on a grand scale as the people of every nation watch.

> His lightning flashes out across the world. The earth sees and trembles. The mountains melt like wax before the LORD, before the LORD of all the earth. The heavens declare his righteousness; every nation sees his glory. For you, O LORD, are most high over all the earth; you are exalted far above all gods.
>
> Psalm 97:4-6, 9 (NLT)

When the sinners all vanish from earth, the godly will be left.

> Let all sinners vanish from the face of the earth; let the wicked disappear forever. As for me—I will praise the LORD! Praise the LORD!

Psalm 104:35 (NLT)

All the wicked of the earth are the scum you skim off;
no wonder I love to obey your decrees!

Psalm 119:119 (NLT)

Bend down the heavens, LORD, and come down. Touch
the mountains so they billow smoke.

Psalm 144:5 (NLT)

The godly will never be disturbed, but the wicked will
be removed from the land.

Proverbs 10:30 (NLT)

Look! The LORD is coming from far away, burning with
anger, surrounded by thick, rising smoke. His lips are
filled with fury; his words consume like fire. His hot
breath pours out like a flood up to the neck of his enemies. He will sift out the proud nations for destruction.
He will bridle them and lead them away to ruin. But the
people of God will sing a song of joy, like the songs at
the holy festivals. You will be filled with joy, as when a
flutist leads a group of pilgrims to Jerusalem, the mountain of the LORD—to the Rock of Israel.

Isaiah 30:27-29 (NLT)

See, the LORD is coming with fire, and his swift chariots roar like a whirlwind. He will bring punishment
with the fury of his anger and the flaming fire of his hot
rebuke.

Isaiah 66:15 (NLT)

The Day of the LORD, judgment day, includes the appearance of a heavenly army, mighty and powerful, led by Jesus on his white horse. Purifying fires burn off the evil, the ungodly, and the planet-wide curse.

> Sound the alarm in Jerusalem! Raise the battle cry on my holy mountain! Let everyone tremble in fear because the day of the LORD is upon us. It is a day of darkness and gloom, a day of thick clouds and deep blackness. Suddenly, like dawn spreading across the mountains, a great and mighty army appears. Nothing like it has been seen before or will ever be seen again. Fire burns in front of them, and flames follow after them.
>
> Joel 2:1-3 (NLT)

> The LORD of Heaven's Armies touches the land and it melts.
>
> Amos 9:5 (NLT)

The LORD is coming to walk on the earth. Purification fires melt the elements beneath his feet as he travels. "Look! The LORD is coming! He leaves his throne in heaven and tramples the heights of the earth. The mountains melt beneath his feet and flow into the valleys like wax in a fire, like water pouring down a hill" (Micah 1:3-4, NLT).

Fire will devour every ungodly person and thing on the planet. All those left after the fire will be kind, humble, and trusting in the LORD. No liars will survive that event. When all ungodly are removed, the rest will live and sleep in peace and safety, and the verses below seem to indicate a reversal of Babel. It was at the Tower of Babel where God confused the people with different languages—causing them to obey his command to scatter throughout the earth. When God reverses this process, all people will be able again to speak the same language and enjoy worshipping the King together. This makes sense in light of the overall removal of the curse caused by mankind's rebellion.

> 'Therefore, be patient,' says the LORD. 'Soon I will stand and accuse these evil nations. For I have decided to gather the kingdoms of the earth and pour out my fiercest anger and fury on them. All the earth will be devoured by the fire of my jealousy. Then I will purify the speech of all people, so that everyone can worship the LORD together. My scattered people who live beyond the rivers of Ethiopia will come to present their offerings. On that day you will no longer need to be ashamed, for you will no longer be rebels against me. I will remove all proud and arrogant people from among you. There will be no more haughtiness on my holy mountain. Those who are left will be the lowly and humble, for it is they who trust in the name of the LORD. The remnant of Israel will do no wrong; they will never tell lies or deceive one another. They will eat and sleep in safety, and no one will make them afraid.'
>
> Zephaniah 3:8-13 (NLT)

Just as God knows the hearts of all and can easily distinguish between Christians in name only and Christians who are truly his people, so it is with the Jewish people. God knows each one by name who is truly committed to him. Notice the connection with the land, used twice in this short passage.

> 'Two-thirds of the people in the land will be cut off and die,' says the LORD. 'But one-third will be left in the land. I will bring that group through the fire and make them pure. I will refine them like silver and purify them like gold. They will call on my name, and I will answer them. I will say, "These are my people," and they will say, "The LORD is our God."'

The LORD is coming. Suddenly. The purification fire of his presence will burn away all evil, and he will cleanse everything Satan soiled.

> Look! I am sending my messenger, and he will prepare the way before me. Then the LORD you are seeking will suddenly come to his Temple. The messenger of the covenant, whom you look for so eagerly, is surely coming," says the LORD of Heaven's Armies. "But who will be able to endure it when he comes? Who will be able to stand and face him when he appears? For he will be like a blazing fire that refines metal, or like a strong soap that bleaches clothes. He will sit like a refiner of silver, burning away the dross. He will purify the Levites, refining them like gold and silver.
>
> Malachi 3:1-3 (NLT)

Purification by Fire: New Testament Support

People with a gentle and humble spirit will one day own and rule the entire earth with the LORD: "God blesses those who are gentle and lowly, for the whole earth will belong to them" (Matthew 5:5, NLT).

In this famous LORD's Prayer, a central focus is that Christians should pray for God's kingdom to come. To some, this might be a novel concept, the kingdom coming here, but that's what he taught. Some say it came in fullness on Pentecost, and in some ways it did. But the rest of the verse indicates that when it does come, God's will, will be done on earth as it is already being done in heaven. The reality is that the church—any church—falls far short of that standard. In addition, some point out that it would be less than prudent for the LORD of lords and King of kings to train us how to pray by including a phrase that would only be appropriate for a few short weeks, and never be fully accomplished. This flies in the face of Jesus' repeated teachings, which confirm that whatever we pray for in his name will be accomplished.

"May your kingdom come soon. May your will be done here on earth, just as it is in heaven" (Matthew 6:10, NLT).

At present, the kingdom of heaven has good people and evil people living together, but when the time for harvesting the good people arrives, evil people will be sorted out and burned.

> Here is another story Jesus told: 'The kingdom of heaven is like a farmer who planted good seed in his field. But that night as everyone slept, his enemy came and planted weeds among the wheat. When the crop began to grow and produce grain, the weeds also grew. The farmer's servants came and told him, 'Sir, the field where you planted that good seed is full of weeds!' 'An enemy has done it!" the farmer exclaimed.' 'Shall we pull out the weeds?' they asked. He replied, 'No, you'll hurt the wheat if you do. Let both grow together until the harvest. Then I will tell the harvesters to sort out the weeds and burn them and to put the wheat in the barn.'
>
> Matthew 13:24-30 (NLT)

Jesus has planted kingdom seeds—people—all over the earth. At harvest time—the end of the current state of earth—Jesus will send out his angels to remove everyone and everything from his kingdom that was not something he planted. Then his kingdom will be pure, beautiful, and enjoyed by all the good seeds (godly people) who then will be full-grown in their new, resurrected, transformed bodies.

> Then, leaving the crowds outside, Jesus went into the house. His disciples said, 'Please explain the story of the weeds in the field.' 'All right,' he said. 'I, the Son of Man,

am the farmer who plants the good seed. The field is the world, and the good seed represents the people of the kingdom. The weeds are the people who belong to the evil one. The enemy who planted the weeds among the wheat is the Devil. The harvest is the end of the world, and the harvesters are the angels. Just as the weeds are separated out and burned, so it will be at the end of the world. I, the Son of Man, will send my angels, and they will remove from my kingdom everything that causes sin and all who do evil, and they will throw them into the furnace and burn them. There will be weeping and gnashing of teeth. Then the godly will shine like the sun in their Father's kingdom. Anyone who is willing to hear should listen and understand!'

Matthew 13:36-43 (NLT)

The "end of days" is described here as a harvest. Note the specific order of things: angels arrive, good people are gathered, and all the wicked people are removed by fiery judgment to purify the kingdom.

Again, the kingdom of heaven is like a fishing net that is thrown into the water and gathers fish of every kind. When the net is full, they drag it up onto the shore, sit down, sort the good fish into crates, and throw the bad ones away. That is the way it will be at the end of the world. The angels will come and separate the wicked people from the godly, throwing the wicked into the fire. There will be weeping and gnashing of teeth. Do you understand? "Yes," they said, "we do."

Matthew 13:47-51 (NLT)

Now listen to this story. A certain landowner planted a vineyard, built a wall around it, dug a pit for pressing out the grape juice, and built a lookout tower. Then he leased the vineyard to tenant farmers and moved to another country. At the time of the grape harvest he sent his servants to collect his share of the crop. But the farmers grabbed his servants, beat one, killed one, and stoned another. So the landowner sent a larger group of his servants to collect for him, but the results were the same. Finally, the owner sent his son, thinking, "Surely they will respect my son." But when the farmers saw his son coming, they said to one another, "Here comes the heir to this estate. Come on, let's kill him and get the estate for ourselves!" So they grabbed him, took him out of the vineyard, and murdered him. When the owner of the vineyard returns, Jesus asked, "what do you think he will do to those farmers?" The religious leaders replied, "He will put the wicked men to a horrible death and lease the vineyard to others who will give him his share of the crop after each harvest."

Matthew 21:33-41 (NLT)

Notice that God is portrayed in the previous passage as a landowner. The landowner's Son gets murdered by the farmers currently tending the land. Then the landowner returns; he had been there for a first coming, so this is the second coming. Then he deals with the wicked people by handing them a death sentence and giving the land to honest, trustworthy people. You could choose to see this illustration just as symbolic, but that would be inconsistent with God's pattern of fulfilling prophecy. All of Jesus' stories have deeper truths hidden within, and it could be that it is the same with this graphic example.

Jesus told them several other stories to illustrate the kingdom. He said, "The kingdom of heaven can be illustrated by the story of a king who prepared a great wedding feast for his son. Many guests were invited, and when the banquet was ready, he sent his servants to notify everyone that it was time to come. But they all refused! So he sent other servants to tell them, 'The feast has been prepared, and choice meats have been cooked. Everything is ready. Hurry!' But the guests he had invited ignored them and went about their business, one to his farm, another to his store. Others seized his messengers and treated them shamefully, even killing some of them. Then the king became furious. He sent out his army to destroy the murderers and burn their city. And he said to his servants, 'The wedding feast is ready, and the guests I invited aren't worthy of the honor. Now go out to the street corners and invite everyone you see.' So the servants brought in everyone they could find, good and bad alike, and the banquet hall was filled with guests. But when the king came in to meet the guests, he noticed a man who wasn't wearing the proper clothes for a wedding. 'Friend,' he asked, 'how is it that you are here without wedding clothes?' And the man had no reply. Then the king said to his aides, 'Bind him hand and foot and throw him out into the outer darkness, where there is weeping and gnashing of teeth.'"

Matthew 22:1-13 (NLT)

Here we have even more biblical reinforcement for the idea that people not responsive to the kingdom's invitation will be removed from the kingdom. Remember that in order to be removed from the kingdom, you must be first located inside it.

Then the servant with the one bag of gold came and said, "Sir, I know you are a hard man, harvesting crops you didn't plant and gathering crops you didn't cultivate. I was afraid I would lose your money, so I hid it in the earth and here it is." But the master replied, "You wicked and lazy servant! You think I'm a hard man, do you, harvesting crops I didn't plant and gathering crops I didn't cultivate? Well, you should at least have put my money into the bank so I could have some interest. Take the money from this servant and give it to the one with the ten bags of gold. To those who use well what they are given, even more will be given, and they will have an abundance. But from those who are unfaithful, even what little they have will be taken away. Now throw this useless servant into outer darkness, where there will be weeping and gnashing of teeth."

Matthew 25:24-30 (NLT)

Those who sit on the assets provided by the King—without focusing on growing his assets—will be removed from the kingdom.

But when the Son of Man comes in his glory, and all the angels with him, then he will sit upon his glorious throne. All the nations will be gathered in his presence, and he will separate them as a shepherd separates the sheep from the goats. He will place the sheep at his right hand and the goats at his left. Then the King will say to those on the right, "Come, you who are blessed by my Father, inherit the kingdom prepared for you from the foundation of the world. For I was hungry, and you fed me. I was thirsty, and you gave me a drink. I was a stranger, and you invited me into your home. I was naked, and you gave me clothing. I was sick, and you cared for me. I was in prison, and you visited me." Then these righteous ones will reply, "LORD, when did we ever see you hungry and feed you? Or thirsty and give you something to drink? Or a stranger and show you hospitality? Or naked and give you clothing? When did we ever see you sick or in prison, and visit you?" And the King will tell them, "I assure you, when you did it to one of the least of these my brothers and sisters, you were doing it to me!" Then the King will turn to those on the left and say, "Away with you, you cursed ones, into the eternal fire prepared for the Devil and his demons! For I was hungry, and you didn't feed me. I was thirsty, and you didn't give me anything to drink. I was a stranger, and you didn't invite me into your home. I was naked, and you gave me no clothing. I was sick and in prison, and you didn't visit me." Then they will reply, "Lord, when did we ever see you hungry or thirsty or a stranger or naked or sick or in prison, and not help you?" And he will answer, "I assure you, when you refused to help the least of these my brothers and sisters, you were refusing to help me." And they will go away into eternal punishment, but the righteous will go into eternal life.

Matthew 25:31-46 (NLT)

As this passage just told us, Jesus is coming with his angelic host to sit on his throne. He plans on gathering all the people from around the world into groups. The wicked group will be sent away. The good group will begin eternal life. "For everyone will be purified with fire" (Mark 9:49, NLT). After worldwide purification and restoration, the feasting will begin.

"People will come from all over the world—from east and west, north and south—to take their places in the kingdom of God. And note this: Some who seem least important now will be the greatest then, and some who are the greatest now will be least important then" (Luke 13:29, NLT).

This Corinthian passage is a key one that helps clarify and distinguish salvation from rewards. Salvation is a gift from God. It can never be earned. But rewards are based on your kingdom activity and on your motivation for that activity.

On the judgment day, fire will reveal what kind of work each builder has done. The fire will show if a person's work has any value. If the work survives, that builder will receive a reward. But if the work is burned up, the builder will suffer great loss. The builder will be saved, but like someone barely escaping through a wall of flames.

1 Corinthians 3:13-15 (NLT)

Some think the earth will be burned up and destroyed, but it's more likely that fire from God will burn off evil impurities—evil people, evil things, and good things done with impure motives—and will be restored to the pristine environment of Eden. This verse supports the restoration theory by specifying that God has plans for the universe— to be part of his Son's inheritance. This includes earth. The word "universe" means a single spoken sentence: God spoke, and it was.

"And now in these final days, he has spoken to us through his Son. God promised everything to the Son as an inheritance, and through the Son he created the universe" (Hebrews 1:2, NLT).

According to the Greek words used here, the earth will be *apollum*: fully destroyed. It will be like *himation* or *ennumi*, which means changing your outer garment or robe. God will declare it *palaioo*, or obsolete, old, worn out, decayed. The *peribolaion* (mantle of the earth, outer covering) will be *helisso*, which means peeled back, folded up, and *allasso* (changed or made different). According to Merriam-Webster's online dictionary, the *peribolaion* is the mantle, the part of earth that lies beneath the crust and above the central core of the earth. It is derived from the word *regolith*, which is the unconsolidated residual or transported material that overlies the solid rock on the earth.

In the beginning, O LORD, you laid the foundations of the earth, and the heavens are the work of your hands. They will perish, but you remain; they will all wear out like a garment. You will roll them up like a robe; like a garment they will be hanged. But you remain the same, and your years will never end.

Hebrews 1:10-12 (NIV)

Finally, these two passages from 2 Peter sum up God's plans. He will purify the world with fire this time rather than water, and the restored earth is part of our eternal future, like the merging of dimensions.

I want to remind you that in the last days scoffers will come, mocking the truth and following their own desires. They will say, "What happened to the promise that Jesus is coming again? From before the times of our ancestors, everything has remained the same since the world was first created." They deliberately forget that God made the heavens by the word of his command, and he brought the earth out from the water and surrounded it with water. Then he used the water to destroy the ancient world with a mighty flood. And by the same word, the present heavens and earth have been stored up for fire. They are being kept for the day of judgment, when ungodly people will be destroyed.

2 Peter 3:3-7 (NLT)

Everything around us is going to be destroyed like this, what holy and godly lives you should live, looking forward to the day of God and hurrying it along. On that day, he will set the heavens on fire, and the elements will melt away in the flames. But we are looking forward to the new heavens and new earth he has promised, a world filled with God's righteousness.

2 Peter 3:11-13 (NLT)

Conclusion

Just as the world was once destroyed by a flood—and still remains, earth is destined for destruction by fire—and will yet remain. Fire will remove all evil and evil people, allowing restoration, resurrection, and rule on *terra-firma*—earth—by the King of kings and LORD of lords.

What Might Be: Dad Visits Lazarus and the Rich Man

There once was a rich man, expensively dressed in the latest fashions, wasting his days in conspicuous consumption. A poor man named Lazarus, covered with sores, had been dumped on his doorstep. All he lived for was to get a meal from scraps off the rich man's table. His best friends were the dogs who came and licked his sores. Then he died, this poor man, and was taken up by the angels to the lap of Abraham. The rich man also died and was buried. In hell and in torment, he looked up and saw Abraham in the distance and Lazarus in his lap. He called out, "Father Abraham, mercy! Have mercy! Send Lazarus to dip his finger in water to cool my tongue. I'm in agony in this fire." But Abraham said, "Child, remember that in your lifetime you got the good things and Lazarus the bad things. It's not like that here. Here he's consoled and you're tormented. Besides, in all these matters there is a huge chasm set between us so that no one can go from us to you even if he wanted to, nor can anyone cross over from you to us." The rich man said, "Then let me ask you, Father: Send him to the house of my father where I have five brothers, so he can tell them the score and warn them so they won't end up here in this place of torment." Abraham answered, 'They have Moses and the Prophets to tell them the score. Let them listen to them." "I know, Father Abraham," he said, "but they're not listening. If someone came back to them from the dead, they would change their ways." Abraham replied, "If they won't listen to Moses and the Prophets, they're not going to be convinced by someone who rises from the dead. "

Luke 16:1931 (The Message)

"Come, Jamie, we are making a visit today."

"A visit? Who are we going to see?"

"Someone you have read about, preached about, someone from Scripture, the new covenant."

"Who is it?"

"There he is now, up on that rocky hill. That is Lazarus, from the parable Jesus told about him and the rich man. Lazarus!"

"Hello, my friend! Is this the newcomer you told me about?"

"Yes. This is Jamie Hemphill. He is from the shadowland. His time was post-flood, and he lived in a small village called Mason, Texas, a state in the United States of America. I told Jamie we were making a visit today, but did not tell to whom it would be. You are his first, so please be patient since this whole process is so new to him. I must go now. Jamie, until we meet again."

"Okay. Thank you. Until then."

"Well, a newcomer! Welcome, Jamie. Actually you are my first newcomer. This is very exciting! Over the last 1,975 years I have enjoyed visits from many people, but never have I been the first stop for a newcomer. Would you like some refreshment?"

"Yes, absolutely. Thank you."

"Malach, would you bring us some refreshment, please?"

"As you wish, LORD. I will return shortly."

"Malach? Is this one of the angelic servants assigned to you, Lazarus?"

"Yes, one of the thirty-three provided by the King. More than many have, far fewer than most, but all are satisfied, and none are jealous—jealousy is a trait not indigenous to the eternal dimension. This group of angelic servants was a serendipity upon my arrival, along with countless other pleasant surprises. The King, as you are only now beginning to discover, is full of these. His love for us runs deep—deeper than we can know. His surprises are constant, daily, and extravagant. But doesn't that match his love? Each day brings new joys, new emotions, and new intellectual and physical challenges. After the first thousand years or so, it becomes evident beyond comprehension that the only thing not here is boredom."

"I've certainly been surprised repeatedly since arriving. And today's surprise for me is that you're a real person, not just an allegorical parable told by Jesus to teach truths in an abstract fashion. I thought you and the rich man were fictional."

"Oh, we're real, all right, though I think Richard wishes he was just an allegory."

"Richard?"

"Richard is the rich man's name in that story. Yes, it was an illustration used by Jesus to teach a truth, but we were—and are—definitely real people. That's the King's way; though it may sound like a made-up anecdote to you, he prefers to communicate truths by using concrete, real-life stories to do so. What else about the story surprised you?"

"Well, I think it was the fact that a dead man wanted some water. Since I knew water was part of my world, I assumed it was not part of yours."

"Why would you make that assumption?"

"I really don't know. Looking back, I guess it was sort of a common opinion that anything tangible or physical was evil for that fact alone. I know it doesn't make sense now, but back then, I guess we never really sat down and thought it through."

"Here is your refreshment, LORD."

"Oh, thank you, Malach. That'll be all for now."

Chapter 5: Resurrection and Our New Body

"God honored the Master's body by raising it from the grave. He'll treat yours with the same resurrection power." (1 Corinthians 6:14, The Message)

One Last Handwritten Note from Dad

At this point, I want to relate a true story about Dad that happened right after he died. I have repeatedly related this event in the years since Dad's death, and those who've heard it walk away shaking their heads, saying, "Wow. What would I have done if that had happened to me? Would I have made the right choice?" But the real reason I am using this illustration is to get you to think about all your relationships right now in light of the resurrection.

Dad changed careers during my time in Abilene Christian University, leaving the school system and going into insurance. As God blessed his efforts, Dad bought an old building on the square downtown and moved his office into it. It was a picturesque place to say the least. The beautiful grounds around the courthouse—right across the street from Dad's office—are filled with huge pecan trees, not unlike those from our own front yard on Live Oak Street.

There's something peaceful, something extra special about small-town squares. The air smells fresher somehow, cleaner in that small-town, all dressed up in a "Sunday-go-to-meeting" kind of atmosphere. That one square block holds a lot of memories for me, not only because Dad was the mayor—a position he was talked into taking because of his love for the community—but also because Dad's office was where he spent most of his time. You could catch him there at all hours, especially during tax season when he worked into the wee hours of the morning to make sure his customers—friends—made the deadline. It didn't matter that people would wait until the week before taxes were due to bring him a shoebox full of assorted receipts, completely unorganized and uncategorized. It only mattered that they still trusted Dad with their private financial information, which they did without reservation. Everyone who knew him considered Dad completely trustworthy.

In a small, dusty closet behind a narrow door in the back of Dad's office was an old safe. I remembered seeing it when Dad bought the building. It looked like one of those old relics brought in by wagon in the late eighteen hundreds, almost as if the building were designed around this artifact rather than the other way around. I guess it was about three feet tall, brown, and as heavy as a three-quarter-ton truck. Literally. I know this because Dad and my brother Kendal told me about trying to move it once, and the weight was so great that they were convinced they would arrive at the office one day soon and discover a square hole in the floor where the one-hundred-plus-year-old peer-and-beam floor had finally given up its lifetime quest of bearing the burden of this one special safe.

But the safe was unique to my brother and me for a very special reason: in our quest for Dad's will after he died, it was in this old safe that we discovered our last handwritten letter from Dad. Now it wasn't what you think. You'd think that when you find a note from your dad addressed to you—when he has gone on to his reward—it would be a long, multi-page letter about his love, his wishes, and his requests, but that's not what we found. Not even close.

Memories fill my head even now as I look at a copy of the front of that envelope I keep in a small display case at my office. It's one of those desktop, glass-enclosed display cases you can buy at craft stores to keep the dust off of the things you pile inside, things that mean something, things that bring tears to your eyes, things that connect you to someone who matters greatly.

My glass case is full of "Dad" stuff. There are his golf shoes that were old, yellowed, and nasty with the seams beginning to come apart, the shoes he wore until he bought some new ones just a few weeks before he died. There's the sign plate from his mayoral desk at the Mason County Courthouse that reads simply "Jamie Hemphill, Mayor." There are a few knickknacks that remind me of him, like a pencil-holder in the shape of a big golf ball, a horseshoe—the symbol that's part of the mascot of the school and the Mason High School Punchers—his business card, and an old, round typewriter eraser with a brush attached to it—the kind they used long before computers. There's the program from his funeral, the corsage I wore to the funeral, and the article—complete with Dad's color picture—from the front page of the San Angelo Standard Times the day after his death. And last, but definitely not least, there's a copy of the front of the sealed envelope we found in that heavy, old safe. The envelope was thick, as if it had several pages inside, and the writing on the front was easily recognizable as Dad's. The memory—even now—of finding these words on that envelope is still overwhelming. Here's what it said:

To: Steve & Kendal

This envelope is not to be opened except in Jamie's presence—if he is no longer living and this is still unopened, then destroy without opening—it is not important.

Dad 1/09/2000

I was in shock. Now what should I do?

I got up. I began pacing back and forth as my brother watched with his mouth wide open. I said, "I can't believe he did this, I just can't believe it. We have to open it. What if it wasn't important then, but it is important now? We have to open it to see."

Isn't it interesting how we can quickly justify what we want to do, even when we know it's really not the right thing to do?

Kendal laughed at my reaction. My brother—almost four years my junior—wisely said, "Now, wait just a minute. Think about it before you do it because once you've opened it, you can't go back."

I stopped. He was right. I really hated to admit it, but he was. Immediately, my mind went into the fast-forward mode to the reunion—my future one with Dad.

"Hello, Dad," I would say as I slowly, tentatively approached him when I catch up with him in the afterlife. I pictured my head hanging low, looking at the floor as I apprehensively ventured closer, nervous that he would be upset at my direct disobedience of the specific instructions he addressed to his two trusted sons. "Sorry, Dad," I would have to say. "We opened that letter you told us not to." Nervous, I think, to hear those words we often heard growing up when we disobeyed him: "Go get my belt."

I couldn't stand it. I couldn't do it. I knew what we had to do. We had to do just what he said to do. We did. We destroyed it. We burned it. Even as the fire caused the contents to curl up and show that it wasn't a trick, it wasn't just a few blank pages filling that envelope from Dad, it really had page after page of handwritten words in Dad's unmistakable writing. We sat there and watched it disintegrate into ashes of nothingness.

But when it was done, I was proud for having done the right thing—when no one was looking. In truth, someone was looking. In fact, lots of "someones," according to the writer of Hebrews:

"We are surrounded by such a huge crowd of witnesses to the life of faith, let us strip off every weight that slows us down, especially the sin that so easily trips us up. And let us run with endurance the race God has set before us" (Hebrews 12:1, NLT).

The next day I went by the Mason National Bank to visit with Connie Stockbridge. Connie took Dad's place as temporary mayor after his death. I told her about the note and my struggle with what to do. She helped me feel good about my decision by saying, "Steven, you did the right thing. Your dad knew what was important, so if he said it wasn't important, I can guarantee you it wasn't important." Connie probably has no idea how much it meant for me to hear those words about Dad.

When I told my wife—Mary Lynn—about the note and how we had burned it, she said, "I can't wait to ask him what was in that envelope!"

I'm glad we destroyed that note, so I can approach Dad with my head up saying, "Hi, Dad. We did what you said. But what was in that note?"

Defeating Death

"The last enemy to be destroyed is death" (1 Corinthians 15:26, NLT).

Our covenant with God made his enemy—Satan—our enemy. It also made our enemy—death—God's enemy. One of Satan's main weapons used to instill fear into our hearts is the fear of death. Jesus came to defeat death, and he did just that. If Jesus' resurrection had been to a ghost-like, non-bodily existence, then death would not have been defeated. But that's not the case. The truth is that death was defeated by Jesus' resurrection, and that death also will be defeated in our own bodily resurrections so you will have a tangible body in eternity.

Is the Physical World Evil?

Some assert that evil lies in the realm of the physical. In other words, to be physical or tangible is to be so engulfed in evil so completely that constant, ongoing relationship with a holy God is impossible. Going even further, they say that we must actually shed the physical, material world completely in order to participate in everlasting life with the King, our Creator.

What's wrong with this line of thought? Only one thing: it's completely unscriptural. Notice what God says after the six days of creation of the physical, material world: "God looked over all he had made, and he saw that it was very good!" (Genesis 1:31, NLT). Everything was tangible, physical, and three dimensional—had length, width, and depth—and it wasn't evil or bad in any way. When the King says something's "good," he declares the truth.

An additional problem with this unfounded theory is that Satan himself was not in tangible, physical form—as far as we could see—yet he was evil: "Open their eyes, so they may turn from darkness to light and from the power of Satan to God. Then they will receive forgiveness for their sins and be given a place among God's people, who are set apart by faith" (Acts 26:18, NLT). Satan's kingdom is a kingdom of darkness or evil even though it isn't physical. Physical properties—according to Scripture—have nothing to do with being good or evil. Good and evil can obviously exist in both realities, both dimensions.

Resurrection Is Motivation for Caring for Our Current Physical Body

"They [our bodies] were made for the LORD, and the LORD cares about our bodies. And God will raise us from the dead by his power, just as he raised our LORD from the dead" (1 Corinthians 6:13-14, NLT).

It's easy to miss what Paul is saying here. What does he teach in this passage about the importance of taking care of our bodies? He teaches that the resurrection should be a motivating factor for taking care of our current physical bodies. If we are destined to be disembodied, floating spirits—as some assert—this would make no sense, but if resurrection is for eternal life—which is the definition of resurrection—then it's easy to connect the dots between taking good care of our current bodies, since they are part of the DNA of our eternal bodies.

Physical Resurrection Was a View Shared by Many Bible Figures

Abraham believed in physical resurrection: "Abraham reasoned that if Isaac died, God was able to bring him back to life again. And in a sense, Abraham did receive his son back from the dead" (Hebrews 11:19, NLT). This verse explains his willingness to kill Isaac even though he knew that Isaac was the son of promise and that through Isaac all the nations of the earth would be blessed.

Job believed in physical resurrection: "But as for me, I know that my Redeemer lives, and he will stand upon the earth at last. And after my body has decayed, yet in my body I will see God! I will see him for myself. Yes, I will see him with my own eyes. I am overwhelmed at the thought!" (Job 19:25-27, NLT). Job fully expected to die, decay, and then be resurrected to see God with his physical eyes.

David believed in physical resurrection: "No wonder my heart is glad, and I rejoice. My body rests in safety. For you will not leave my soul among the dead or allow your holy one to rot in the grave. You will show me the way of life, granting me the joy of your presence and the pleasures of living with you forever" (Psalm 16:9-11, NLT).

Although part of this passage is pointed to in the prophetic discussions of Jesus and is definitely pointing to the resurrection of the Savior, note here that King David is also specifically talking about his own body. He held the personal belief that he would rise from the grave in a resurrected life and live with God forever.

Abraham, Job, and David all believed in a physical resurrection. Jesus's friend Lazarus believed in the physical resurrection—he experienced it. Jesus demonstrated the resurrection and the fact that it was physical and literal. "The earth shook, rocks split apart, and tombs opened. The bodies of many godly men and women who had died were raised from the dead. They left the cemetery after Jesus' resurrection, went into the holy city of Jerusalem, and appeared to many people" (Matthew 27:51-53, NLT).

This verse from Matthew 27 even reveals that many others were resurrected when Jesus was. Now for the tough question: do you believe in the resurrection? I pray that by the time you finish this chapter you do believe in a real, tangible, permanent, physical resurrection.

Resurrection Teachings and Examples in Scripture

Notice how baptism is specifically tied to the resurrection: "Have you forgotten that when we were joined with Christ Jesus in baptism, we joined him in his death? For we died and were buried with Christ by baptism. And just as Christ was raised from the dead by the glorious power of the Father, now we also may live new lives" (Romans 6:3-4, NLT).

We can't live long underwater, without air. We are buried in the waters of baptism in the likeness of the death of Jesus and his burial in the tomb. Then we come up a new person, renewed by the Spirit of God, fresh and ready to walk a new life of faith. Note also that you can't bury someone with a few drops—as in sprinkling—burial requires being completely submerged.

We are often deceived into thinking that the permanent resting place of our physical body is the grave, but that's not God's opinion: "The LORD himself will come down from heaven with a commanding shout, with the voice of the archangel, and with the trumpet call of God. First, the Christians who have died will rise from their graves" (1 Thessalonians 4:16, NLT).

If your physical DNA isn't a permanent part of your eternity, there is no need for the graves to open and give up the dead. I also think it's interesting to note here that the Greek word used in this passage for the English word "rise" literally means to stand upright again. Pretty graphic picture, isn't it?

Jesus Rose From the Grave

"After Jesus rose from the dead early on Sunday morning, the first person who saw him was Mary Magdalene, the woman from whom he had cast out seven demons" (Mark 16:9, NLT).

The Dead Rich Man Wanted Water

"The rich man shouted, 'Father Abraham, have some pity! Send Lazarus over here to dip the tip of his finger in water and cool my tongue. I am in anguish in these flames'" (Luke 16:24, NLT).

The rich man wanted Abraham to send Lazarus to simply dip his finger into water and touch it to his tongue. What does a dead man want with water if his body isn't physical?

Scripture Says Our New Body Will Be Like Jesus' Resurrection Body

"He will take our weak mortal bodies and change them into glorious bodies like his own, using the same power with which he will bring everything under his control" (Philippians 3:21, NLT).

There Are Bodies in Heaven

"There are also bodies in the heavens and bodies on the earth. The glory of the heavenly bodies is different from the glory of the earthly bodies" (1 Corinthians 15:40, NLT).

Resurrection of Earth Is Also Promised

"Then times of refreshment will come from the presence of the LORD, and he will again send you Jesus, your appointed Messiah. For he must remain in heaven until the time for the final restoration of all things, as God promised long ago through his holy prophets" (Acts 3:20-22, NLT).

"Against its will, all creation was subjected to God's curse. But with eager hope, the creation looks forward to the day when it will join God's children in glorious freedom from death and decay" (Romans 8:20-21, NLT).

"And the one sitting on the throne said, 'Look, I am making everything new!' And then he said to me, 'Write this down, for what I tell you is trustworthy and true'" (Revelation 21:5, NLT).

Even the Sea Will Give Up the Dead

"The sea gave up its dead, and death and the grave gave up their dead. And all were judged according to their deeds" (Revelation 20:13, NLT).

If your physical DNA isn't a permanent part of your eternal body, there's no need for the bodies in the sea to be removed.

Seeds Are the Metaphor of Choice Describing Our Eternal Bodies

Paul wrote that some would be confused about the resurrection. He was concerned that the idea of a literal, physical resurrection would be attacked or dismissed, so he explained it thoroughly here in 1 Corinthians. Notice how he called people foolish if they questioned whether or not we would have a body in eternity:

> Someone may ask, 'How will the dead be raised? What kind of bodies will they have?' What a foolish question!

When you put a seed into the ground, it doesn't grow into a plant unless it dies first. And what you put in the ground is not the plant that will grow, but only a bare seed of wheat or whatever you are planting. Then God gives it the new body he wants it to have. A different plant grows from each kind of seed. Similarly there are different kinds of flesh—one kind for humans, another for animals, another for birds, and another for fish. There are also bodies in the heavens and bodies on the earth. The glory of the heavenly bodies is different from the glory of the earthly bodies. The sun has one kind of glory, while the moon and stars each have another kind. And even the stars differ from each other in their glory. It is the same way with the resurrection of the dead. Our earthly bodies are planted in the ground when we die, but they will be raised to live forever.

1 Corinthians 15:35-43 (NLT)

To help illustrate our eternal body, he uses the perfect metaphor: a seed. When you plant corn, the seed dies—like we do—and a corn stalk grows from it. The new plant has everything the original seed has, but that's not all. It's now taller, bigger, and contains lots of seeds identical to the original, but the original seed is recognizable in the plant that came from it.

I like to think of it in terms of recognizing a young man or woman you knew when they were children, but haven't seen in a long time. You immediately see similarities to how you remember them, but they are now taller, their bodies more fully developed. They've grown up. You mentally connect their young body from your memory bank to this new, better one, and in the future you will be able to recognize them from the mental picture you now carry in your mind.

Then in verse 44, Paul puts a punctuation on his assertion about our having a permanent physical body: "They are buried as natural human bodies, but they will be raised as spiritual bodies. For just as there are natural bodies, there are also spiritual bodies" (1 Corinthians 15:44, NLT). The Greek word for "spiritual bodies" here is "pneumatiko." The proper definition in light of all these passages comes through in what this word means: concretely supernatural. In eternity, we will have real, tangible, concrete bodies that will also be completely supernatural in terms of being immortal or eternal.

Butterflies

Butterflies are probably the best example in nature that reminds us of the future reality of physical resurrection. In fact, I can't think of a better example in creation than this one. The ugly, slimy, dirty, physically limited caterpillar is buried in a cocoon, and in a short time emerges as a beautiful, colorful, dainty, ornate flying creature we know as a butterfly. Think how limited the worm is in comparison to the freedom experienced by the soaring butterfly. And notice that the original worm is changed, enhanced, and improved in the redesigned butterfly and that they share the same DNA.

Springtime Is a Yearly Example

All of our lives, every year without fail, the grass around us turns brown as though it were dead, many trees lose their leaves causing the same illusion, and the winter weather works its way into our weary bones until we sometimes even begin to feel dead, tired, or used up. But spring always follows, and although a child might see the resurrection of spring as almost a miracle, we take for granted the renewal, restoration, and the revitalization of the trees, grass, and plants. Now add the fresh new flowers, the birth of many new animals, and the feeling of refreshment and joy that invigorates us at that time of year, and springtime gives us a new outlook on life. This new attitude pushes the ugly cold of winter of the past few months right out of our minds. I believe this is meant to give us a regular, yearly glimpse of the future: restoration, resurrection, and heaven.

Three Physical Bodies Currently in Heaven: Enoch, Elijah, and Jesus

Enoch walked with God and God took him: "Enoch walked with God; then he was no more, because God took him away" (Genesis 5:24, NIV).

Elijah went up in a chariot of fire carried by a whirlwind: "As they were walking along and talking, suddenly a chariot of fire appeared, drawn by horses of fire. It drove between the two men, separating them, and Elijah was carried by a whirlwind into heaven" (2 Kings 2:11, NLT).

Jesus ascended from the Mount of Olives with the disciples watching in the same body that he invited them to touch and feel: "When he had led them out to the vicinity of Bethany, he lifted up his hands and blessed them. While he was blessing them, he left them and was taken up into heaven" (Luke 24:50-51, NIV).

Many Christians Are Confused About Resurrection

It saddens me to know that many Christians—perhaps even a majority—don't believe in the resurrection. They believe in an afterlife, but not in the resurrection. The definition of resurrection is a dead body coming back to life. Period. Anything less is not a resurrection. Isn't it important enough to spend a little time gaining a correct, biblical understanding of? Let's explore it together.

Resurrection comes from the Middle English word *resurrecioun*. The Late Latin word is resurrection, or *resurrectio*, the act of rising from the dead. The root is *resurgere*, to rise from the dead or to rise again.

What comes to mind when you read those definitions? And more importantly, how does this fit with the biblical thought of resurrection? Is it an ethereal, ghost-like, see-through-body existence? No. Not even close.

The Ascension of Jesus

"Jesus led them to Bethany, and lifting his hands to heaven, he blessed them. While he was blessing them, he left them and was taken up to heaven" (Luke 24:50-51, NLT).

Sometimes it's insightful to note what isn't said. This is one of those passages. Let's make note of what doesn't happen here.

Some Christians live as though it read, "While he was blessing them, he left them, and he also left his temporary human skin and bones. His spirit was taken up to heaven." The problem is that this is not what it says. His skin and bones went up with him. Jesus's skin and bones rose up from the grave and into the sky. His physical body was completely intact; the same physical body he worked so hard to convince the disciples was real, tangible, restored, and resurrected rose up into the clouds of the sky. He didn't leave any part of it behind.

Redefining Resurrection

Resurrection isn't just a new description of death; it's victory over death, coming back to life, dead tissue becoming living tissue again. Resurrection was originally preached as an eternal existence, not just a Christian brand of ghostly afterlife. People understood perfectly that resurrection meant that their physical body would come back to life after being dead. Today's "Christian" idea that resurrection could mean anything less is simply a lie from Satan. Resurrection is to be followed by transformation into an immortal. This is the scriptural truth that many have ignored or attempted to re-define.

Why is my language not clear to you? Because you are unable to hear what I say. You belong to your father, the devil, and you want to carry out your father's desire. He was a murderer from the beginning, not holding to the truth, for there is no truth in him. When he lies, he speaks his native language, for he is a liar and the father of lies. Yet because I tell the truth, you do not believe me!

John 8:43-45 (NIV)

Resurrection is victory over death. This is a message that's been hard to accept since it was first preached: "While Paul was waiting for them in Athens, he was greatly distressed to see that the city was full of idols. So he reasoned in the synagogue with the Jews and the God-fearing Greeks, as well as in the marketplace day by day with those who happened to be there. A group of Epicurean and Stoic philosophers began to dispute with him. Some of them asked, 'What is this babbler trying to say?' Others remarked, 'He seems to be advocating foreign gods.' They said this because Paul was preaching the good news about Jesus and the resurrection." (Acts 17:16-18, NIV).

Resurrection, then transformation, is the scriptural truth that many have ignored or attempted to redefine, but their new definition doesn't match Scripture.

I declare to you, brothers, that flesh and blood cannot inherit the kingdom of God, nor does the perishable inherit the imperishable. Listen, I tell you a mystery: We will not all sleep, but we will all be changed—in a flash, in the twinkling of an eye, at the last trumpet. For the trumpet will sound, the dead will be raised imperishable, and we will be changed. For the perishable must clothe itself with the imperishable, and the mortal with immortality. When the perishable has been clothed with the imperishable, and the mortal with immortality, then the saying that is written will come true: "Death has been swallowed up in victory."

1 Corinthians 15:50-54 (NIV)

This teaches that our physical bodies will be changed or transformed into a body that will be eternal. Apparently, the transformation will change our flesh and blood body—which cannot live forever—into an immortal body that *can* live forever. The DNA from the first body is not eliminated, it's changed. This passage is the biblical definition of victory over death, and it comes in two forms. Dead people in the grave will come back to life in their original, physical form before being transformed into an immortal, and living people simply skip the grave and undergo the same transformation. It sounds simple, and Scripture teaches it like it's a simple process, but Satan has been quite successful in convincing the masses—including many Christians—that this truth is a lie. But isn't this what he's best at?

Rising from the Grave

What is it that will rise from the grave? Dead bodies.

> Brothers, we do not want you to be ignorant about those who fall asleep, or to grieve like the rest of men, who have no hope. We believe that Jesus died and rose again and so we believe that God will bring with Jesus those who have fallen asleep in him. According to the LORD's own word, we tell you that we who are still alive, who are left till the coming of the LORD, will certainly not precede those who have fallen asleep. For the LORD himself will come down from heaven, with a loud command, with the voice of the archangel and with the trumpet call of God, and the dead in Christ will rise first. After that, we who are still alive and are left will be caught up together with them in the clouds to meet the LORD in

the air. And so we will be with the LORD forever. Therefore encourage each other with these words.

1 Thessalonians 4:13-18 (NIV)

Does God want you to be uninformed about eternity and dead Christians? No. Does this mean he wants you to be interested in it, informed about it, and study Scripture to know more about it? Yes. Why would this be important? To get us excited about it. Why? To spur us on to evangelism—taking other people into eternal life with us.

This says that when Jesus comes back, all the dead Christians will come with him. What would be the purpose of them coming back here? Because "here" would be a restored earth. The King wants to show off his perfect and good creation—restored to perfection. He wants us all to enjoy it, just like he wanted from the beginning.

Where are they coming from? Probably paradise—the intermediate heaven.

What part of the dead Christian comes with Jesus as he returns to the earth? First of all, the soul and spirit would return to be united with the original body that was temporarily separated from the mortal physical body. (An interesting side note comes from Revelation 6:9-11, where the King asked the martyred saints to wait a little longer and put on some clothing while they wait. You can't hang clothing on a spirit or ghost, so there could possibly be an intermediate form of tangible body during the interim between death and resurrection.)

And I assure you that the time is coming, indeed it's here now, when the dead will hear my voice—the voice of the Son of God. And those who listen will live. The Father has life in himself, and he has granted that same life-giving power to his Son. And he has given him authority to judge everyone because he is the Son of Man. Don't be so surprised! Indeed, the time is coming when all the dead in their graves will hear the voice of God's Son, and they will rise again.

John 5:25-29, (NLT)

Dead people in the grave will hear. "A time is coming when all who are in their graves will hear his voice" (John 5:28, NIV).

What is the significance of this? Their dead bodies will be resurrected and reunited with their soul and spirit.

"We would rather be away from these earthly bodies, for then we will be at home with the LORD" (2 Corinthians 5:8-9, NLT).

What They Thought When Jesus Died

When Jesus died, nobody said, "Oh well, he's in heaven with God now" or "He's definitely the Messiah we hoped for!" Here's what the disciples said: "We had hoped he was the Messiah who had come to rescue Israel" (Luke 24:21, NLT).

So what did his death mean? Defeat. Game over. Hope crushed. They had bet on the wrong horse. They had thought he was the King, and the prayer he taught them had helped confirm it, so nothing made sense anymore.

What had Jesus taught them to pray? He taught them to pray for the kingdom to come to earth "as it is in heaven."

What Did Resurrection Mean to the Disciples?

With this in mind, what did the resurrection mean to them? Victory was assured. If the King can defeat death, the opposition is hopeless, the enemy would be crushed, and the opposition was wrong about Jesus. Jesus is King. Now the prayer he taught them did make sense, and the kingdom would come one day to earth. They just didn't know when. But the "when" no longer mattered because they were sure now that it would—it was just a matter of time, and God has an unlimited supply of that.

The first few verses in Acts 1 record the continual appearance of the post-resurrection King to the disciples with one main topic on his lips: heaven. And after forty days of teachings from the King that focused on heaven, they just had one question. This one question was basically, "Is the kingdom coming to earth right now?" The answer Jesus gave them further confirmed that the kingdom will come here. He didn't say, "just kidding" or "changed my mind" or even "That was just a symbolic prayer not meant to be taken literally." He confirmed it by saying, "Only the Father knows the date and time."

What Will Our Body Be Like?

Our body will be like the resurrected body of our LORD: "Our citizenship is in heaven. And we eagerly await a Savior from there, the LORD Jesus Christ, who, by the power that enables him to bring everything under his control, will transform our lowly bodies so that they will be like his glorious body" (Philippians 3:20-21, NIV).

What was his body like? What could his body do? It could disappear in one place and appear in another; it could pass through walls or locked doors; it could ingest food and drink; it was real, tangible, appearing completely physical, but it was immortal—it was transformed after having been to the Father. He carried the identifying marks from his physical death on the cross—these wounds connected his temporary body with his immortal body. These verses confirm these facts.

> "By this time they were nearing Emmaus and the end of their journey. Jesus acted as if he were going on, but they begged him, 'Stay the night with us, since it is getting late.' So he went home with them. As they sat down to eat, he took the bread and blessed it. Then he broke it and gave it to them. Suddenly, their eyes were opened, and they recognized him. And at that moment he disappeared!"
>
> Luke 24:28-31 (NLT)

That Sunday evening the disciples were meeting behind locked doors because they were afraid of the Jewish leaders. Suddenly, Jesus was standing there among them! "Peace be with you,' he said. As he spoke, he showed them the wounds in his hands and his side.'

John 20:19-20 (NLT)

For we know that when this earthly tent we live in is taken down (that is, when we die and leave this earthly body), we will have a house in heaven, an eternal body made for us by God himself and not by human hands. We grow weary in our present bodies, and we long to put on our heavenly bodies like new clothing. For we will put on heavenly bodies; we will not be spirits without bodies. While we live in these earthly bodies, we groan and sigh, but it's not that we want to die and get rid of these bodies that clothe us. Rather, we want to put on our new bodies so that these dying bodies will be swallowed up by life.

2 Corinthians 5:1-5 (NLT)

The whole group was startled and frightened, thinking they were seeing a ghost! "Why are you frightened?" he asked. "Why are your hearts filled with doubt? Look at my hands. Look at my feet. You can see that it's really me. Touch me and make sure that I am not a ghost, because ghosts don't have bodies, as you see that I do." As he spoke, he showed them his hands and his feet. Still they stood there in disbelief, filled with joy and wonder. Then he asked them, "Do you have anything here to eat?" They gave him a piece of broiled fish, and he ate it as they watched.

Luke 24:37-43 (NLT)

And even we Christians, although we have the Holy Spirit within us as a foretaste of future glory, also groan to be released from pain and suffering. We, too, wait anxiously for that day when God will give us our full rights as his children, including the new bodies he has promised us.

Romans 8:23 (NLT)

"Dear woman, why are you crying?" the angels asked her. "Because they have taken away my LORD," she replied, "and I don't know where they have put him." She turned to leave and saw someone standing there. It was Jesus, but she didn't recognize him. "Dear woman, why are you crying?" Jesus asked her. "Who are you looking for?" She thought he was the gardener. "Sir," she said, "if you have taken him away, tell me where you have put him, and I will go and get him." "Mary!" Jesus said. She turned to him and cried out, "Rabboni!" (which is Hebrew for 'Teacher'). "Don't cling to me," Jesus said, "for I haven't yet ascended to the Father. But go find my brothers and tell them that I am ascending to my Father and your Father, to my God and your God. "

John 20:13-17 (NLT)

From all appearances, our body will be just like his, physical in appearance, but immortal in nature. You will be you—otherwise it won't be you that goes into eternal life. You will be recognizable and physical, but you will also be immortal, having a physical body transformed into one that will live forever. According to the Holy Scriptures—where all truth is revealed—this is what we have to look forward to.

What Might Be: Seeing What God Sees

"Hello, my guide and friend! What's in store for me today?"

"Hello, Jamie. Well, well, aren't we excited for our lessons these days!"

"I can't help it! I'm learning to expect the unexpected, to anticipate the wonderful, to crave the unreachable, the unbelievable, the unattainable. I've learned that they're all possible here! What are we doing today? Where are we going? Who will I get to meet? Will it be Adam? Enoch? Moses? Paul? I can't wait to see who it will be!"

"We will meet no one new, not today."

"No one? But why? Do I get to go back to one of the elect that I've already met? Lazarus? Samuel? Peter? Did I miss something in my previous interaction with them that I must learn before moving on?"

"No, friend. The King is completely pleased with your joy in each experience and the growth you have shown from all the interaction with all those you have met. Today you are to have a special treat, an experience that will guide your walk, enhance your prayers as you talk to the King, and lead you deeper in your understanding of his love. Today we peel off another layer from your immortal eyes to reveal another dimension that you will now be allowed to view. In order for you to understand what you are about to see, let me show you some background from the guidebook.

"There are many insights from the Old Testament, but I want to focus primarily today on the New, so I'll just mention one from the Old that begins to give you a glimpse of where we're headed. Keep in mind as we discuss these passages from the guidebook that this entire exercise is designed specifically to prepare you for what you are about to see. Note the references in these passages that refer to light and darkness. This first one is from one of the Psalm: Psalm 36:9 "For you are the fountain of life, the light by which we see." "The King created light as a staple of life because he is light. No darkness at all is in him.

"This first reference in the new covenant is from a spiritual warfare passage that you are already quite familiar with, but notice now the reference to darkness as the current state of the world: 'For our struggle is not against flesh and blood, but against the rulers, against the authorities, against the powers of this dark world and against the spiritual forces of evil in the heavenly realms.'

"Paul goes on in the second letter to the Corinthians to reveal Satan's current position as leader of these dark forces, the one working to keep people from seeing the Light of God: 'Satan, who is the god of this world, has blinded the minds of those who don't believe. They are unable to see the glorious light of the Good News.'

"Who is the Light of God? Jesus. 'I have come as a light to shine in this dark world, so that all who put their trust in me will no longer remain in the dark.'

"When they were about to arrest him and murder him, Jesus confirmed that darkness is the current power over the planet: 'Why didn't you arrest me in the Temple? I was there every day. But this is your moment, the time when the power of darkness reigns.'

"Jesus came here for the explicit purpose of establishing a 'beachhead,' so to speak, to begin to retake the land that Satan had captured. His purpose was to reveal the light of God to the nations of the world through his sacrifice: 'He is a light to reveal God to the nations.'

"For now, death casts its shadow on the land, but he will return and defeat death for everyone. This will happen at the resurrection: 'The people who sat in darkness have seen a great light. And for those who lived in the land where death casts its shadow, a light has shined.'

"The resurrection of Jesus cracked open a fissure into our eternal future, and as we peek into that fissure we can see that all the godly will be raised back to life. The transformed body they will possess will be immortal. Jesus opened that crack so darkness would begin to be displaced by the kingdom of Light: 'The Word gave life to everything that was created, and his life brought light to everyone. The light shines in the darkness, and the darkness can never extinguish it.'

"The host was most surprised by the majority response to this new revelation. Most people chose darkness over light: 'God's light came into the world, but people loved the darkness more than the light, for their actions were evil. All who do evil hate the light and refuse to go near it for fear their sins will be exposed. But those who do what is right come to the light so others can see that they are doing what God wants.'

"Jesus is the light that leads to life, eternal life: 'Jesus spoke to the people once more and said, "I am the light of the world. If you follow me, you won't have to walk in darkness, because you will have the light that leads to life."'

"The other surprise for the disciples came in the realization that the King loved Gentiles as much as he did the Jews. Most of them had a very difficult time with this, but the Light of the kingdom was destined to be available to all: 'I am sending you to the Gentiles to open their eyes, so they may turn from darkness to light and from the power of Satan to God.'

"You know of the battle that is raging in the unseen, the battle between God and Satan. This is truly a battle of light and darkness. Winning the battle takes faith: 'Put your trust in the light while there is still time; then you will become children of the light.'

"Winning the battle means turning from darkness to light—Jesus. 'While I am here in the world, I am the light of the world.'

"In our dimension, we were all amazed that no one could recognize Jesus because it was so obvious to us. Then the King informed us of the dimensional limits that were placed temporarily on all humans: you were prevented from seeing it. You could not see the light that burst from his presence, his countenance, his mouth as he spoke. You could not see the splash of colors that filled the hillside as he said, 'The meek shall inherit the earth.' You could not smell the rainbow colors that filled the sky as the King's Son leaned back, glancing up at the sky and said, 'Peacemakers will be called sons of God.' The fragrance was staggering, almost intoxicating to us. The truth of the real world was leaking out into your sin-sick one, and we were sure it would change things overnight.

"Change things? Yes, most definitely. Overnight? Hardly. Almost 2,000 years later, evil is still the dominating banner waving. Ugliness still rules. Pain and death are still present, but not for long. The fissure will soon burst. And the light from the real world will invade and conquer. But the King is patient, wanting on the rest of the elect to come to faith, repentance, obedience. 'You are the light of the world—like a city on a hilltop that cannot be hidden.'

"Resurrection? Yes. It's coming. But Satan has worked most diligently to disguise and discount the prophetic act that is the first step in each individual's resurrection. Each person must join ranks with the army of the King. They must wear the golden seal that empowers their position and enables their authority to see truly and to be seen clearly in the real world—the world of the King. Each must join Christ Jesus in his death in order to be commissioned in his power: 'Have you forgotten that when we were joined with Christ Jesus in baptism, we joined him in his death? For we died and were buried with Christ by baptism. And just as Christ was raised from the dead by the glorious power of the Father, now we also may live new lives.'"

"I think I understand better. It's coming into clearer focus. It's like my mind is finally wrapping itself around this old truth, this old commandment to now know its true significance."

"Yes. And now you are ready to have the optical layer removed that prevents you from seeing the reality of this dimension. Please lean your head back, open your eyes wide, and say,

'Jesus, LORD and King; my life and heart and strength I bring; open my eyes, remove the veil that clouds my sight and keeps me from seeing the truth in the land of darkness that will one day be filled with your light.'

"Now blink twice and look through your portal at the world. Tell me what you see."

When Jamie looked at the world, it was at first like waking from a deep sleep. The blurriness from his past clouded his vision, but then he blinked, and it was like stepping into a dream. Although everything could be seen in perfect clarity, it was obvious who the good people—the saved people—were. They shone like stars. They glowed as the walked, drove, or rode in airplanes. Some planes were riding in total darkness, but others glowed in the sky. Jamie noticed one that had so much light streaming out that it was as if there were huge floodlights pointed out each window. That knowledge flooded his mind: this plane was full of Christians on a mission trip to Africa.

Then he noticed lights appearing at various places around the planet, flickering into existence to bring light to invade the darkness. Then he looked closer—his eyes were now able to zoom like a camera lens—bringing one of these new flickers into perfect clarity. What had just happened? What caused a dark area to light up? What changed the dark person into a mini-me of Jesus? At first he couldn't tell. Then he saw a drop of something. Was it red, a drop of blood? No, was it red water? No, it was an explosion of water and blood. It was just as Jesus had explained to Nicodemus, "No one can enter the kingdom of heaven without being born of spirit and water." It looked like a bomb had exploded just below the surface of pools of water all around the world. Then he saw dozens of them, splashing light into existence, bringing hope to dark parts of the planet.

He refocused, adjusting his zoom to see a larger area of the planet. He was quickly adapting to his improved vision and all the detail that could be gleaned from the data that flowed into his head rapid-fire—like a supercomputer coming online for the first time and moving from inanimate object to useful existence. What were these splashing bombs of light that changed entire regions of the planet from a hopeless void into a beachhead of hope for the future? Realization startled him like a tidal wave: These explosions of light were people of faith who were joining Christ in the likeness of his death—they were being baptized.

Jamie looked at his teacher, who was beaming with excitement, and smiled. Then he turned his attention back to the planet. He adjusted his new eyesight to, at first, take in whole regions, then further back to see continents. Now the Scriptures made sense. Verses throughout the Bible began to trickle through the corridors of his mind. Descriptions that he had always taken metaphorically were real, each and every one. Each phrase helped unveil a new truth—a literal reality—that was now as obvious as the horns on a goat. "This dark world," "as a light that shines in the darkness," and "The kingdom of light advances" all made sense now. They were truth. God's word is truth. And the truth is that God's kingdom of light is going to rule the planet. Forever. It's just a matter of time.

And the King has all the time in the world—and then some.

Chapter 6: Connecting Eternity, Heaven, and New Earth

"The new heavens and new earth that I am making will stand firm before me. God's Decree"

(Isaiah 66:22, The Message).

Dad Was a Math Teacher

Dad was a coach and a math teacher for many years. Without good math skills, life is much more difficult. Math teachers connect the dots (math dots, like two plus two equals four) and teach others to do the same. Dad believed what he did helped others, and his students loved him. We could hardly go anywhere that someone didn't recognize Dad and shout a friendly greeting. Those conversations I witnessed repeatedly during my early years of going to town with Dad often ended with the ex-student saying, "I'm using what you taught me, Mr. Hemphill. Thanks. Good to see you, sir." They always seemed to treat Dad with respect and often even with admiration. Me too.

Dad's math skills helped him in many phases of his life, but the main one was how he used that knowledge to count the cost. He taught students to understand the basics of math so their whole life would be enhanced, and he taught my brother and me that counting the cost would keep us on the most important track, the one leading to heaven.

Jesus teaches us to count the cost of discipleship and even has a story about someone who started a building project only to discover he was unable to finish because he ran out of money (Luke 14:28-33). How embarrassing. It's important to count the cost on earthly projects, but that doesn't compare to the vital necessity of counting the cost of missing eternity with God.

Scripture commands us to focus on eternity (Colossians 3:1). Most of us are disobedient in this respect. Let's remedy that. It's easy to do. All we need to do is connect the dots—add things up and see what the total is. If we can do this, then understanding eternity might just be as easy as adding up a list of numbers to get the total. And once you've seen it, it can change your life forever. It's like eating peanut butter all your life and then getting your first rib-eye steak. After that, peanut butter is okay, but it just doesn't satisfy anymore because the knowledge of a juicy steak gives you an inner hunger for something better. Heaven is better, and we need to learn to hunger for it.

The Bible talks about eternity, heaven, the kingdom, the church, and an eternal new earth. Let's see if we can connect the dots—add up the numbers in this list—and come up with a cumulative total that helps these terms converge to make more sense, giving us a truer vision of the realities of heaven. Maybe by doing this we can get excited about our eternal future—excited enough to get busy taking others with us.

Living on a Destroyed Planet

Are you aware that you currently live on a destroyed planet?

"God made the heavens by the word of his command, and he brought the earth up from the water and surrounded it with water. Then he used the water to destroy the world with a mighty flood" (2 Peter 3:5-6, NLT).

God destroyed it with a worldwide flood. He promised Noah—with a rainbow as the sign—that he would never destroy it with water again, but he never said he wouldn't destroy it some other way. The point here is that in God's view, destruction doesn't mean annihilation. It means cleansing, removing evil, and purification.

God Plans to Destroy It Again

"The heavens and the earth that now exist are being preserved by the same command of God, in order to be destroyed by fire. They are being kept for the day when godless people will be judged and destroyed" (2 Peter 3:7, TEV).

Destruction by flood didn't mean annihilation, so couldn't destruction by fire be interpreted the same way? The last part of this verse could have read, "Earth is being kept for the day when all physical matter everywhere will be annihilated and removed forever," but it doesn't. In fact, note that it specifies what will be destroyed, and that destruction has nothing to do with godly people—it's reserved for the godless.

"The day of the LORD will come like a thief. The heavens will disappear with a roar; the elements will be destroyed by fire, and the earth and everything in it will be laid bare" (2 Peter 3:10, NIV).

The day of judgment will cause the earth to be "laid bare," just as it was after the flood washed the earth clean.

God's Land Plans

"For only the godly will live in the land, and those with integrity will remain in it. But the wicked will be removed from the land, and the treacherous will be uprooted" (Proverbs 2:21-22, NLT).

God plans for the wicked to be removed from the land. People with evil, treacherous hearts will not be allowed to remain. But the godly—all those who are truly committed to the LORD—will inherit the land for eternity. David, the man after God's own heart, wrote in many a Psalm that the land was to be a permanent inheritance of the godly. Psalm 37 is just one example. I'll cover this chapter later in detail, but note that David repeatedly specified here that the godly will end up with the land.

Do you think David was just talking allegorically or metaphorically? Then consider the words of Jesus. As he taught the crowds from what would become the Mount of Beatitudes, his subject was the kingdom of heaven. Notice how the earth and the land are such a vital part of and is inexorably tied into that subject: "One day as he saw the crowds gathering, Jesus went up on the mountainside and sat down. His disciples gathered around him, and he began to teach them. 'God blesses those who are poor and realize their need for him, for the kingdom of heaven is theirs. God blesses those who are humble, for they will inherit the whole earth'" (Matthew 5:1-5, NLT).

Then in the next chapter, he goes even further. He instructs his disciples to pray for the kingdom to come to earth just like it now exists in heaven: "Pray like this: Our Father in heaven, may your name be kept holy. May your kingdom come soon. May your will be done on earth, as it is in heaven" (Matthew 6:9-10, NLT).

For those who say that the kingdom already came (in one sense, it did), notice this commonly overlooked detail: The instructions from Jesus to pray for the kingdom to come soon is so that God's will can be done on earth just as it is now done in heaven. How is God's will done in the unseen? It's done perfectly, completely, and immediately. When God issues an edict, the angels don't pull out their BlackBerrys and say, "I can do that next week." They immediately set out to accomplish it. How does the church fulfill God's commands? Perfectly, immediately, or completely? No. The church—as wonderful as it is—doesn't even come close. The church is a mere shadow of how God's commands will be fulfilled here some day.

The Greek word used for "kingdom" here in Matthew literally means "his reign" or "realm," and the Greek word used for "come" literally means to "bring." Put the phrase together, and you end up with a prayer for the King to literally bring his realm of reign, his reality, to earth. Then you can better understand the why: so his will is done on earth just like it's done in heaven.

Jesus is God, Immanuel, God with us, God incarnate. He really only gave them this one main prayer, and he knew it would be recorded. He knew it would be quoted. He knew it would be distributed for centuries to come and billions would read and learn from it. Do you honestly think that he gave them this little phrase just to be applicable to the few dozen who would know it and pray it for just a few weeks or months until Pentecost? It's possible, but not probable. However, if he and the Father had plans to one day bring their kingdom to earth, restore what Satan destroyed, and eventually upgrade all creation to a new heaven and a new earth, a prayer like this would make sense, wouldn't it?

Maybe we should be fervently praying that prayer today. Wouldn't it be great if his will was done on earth just as it is in heaven? I believe it will. And I'm asking you to consider this possibility based on the specific, overall Bible teachings about heaven sprinkled throughout the Holy Scriptures.

Five Earths in Scripture

I have discovered that most people—including Christians—are completely unaware that Scripture specifically discusses five earths.

Original earth was first, a perfect creation without bad smells, stickers, thorns, or bad weather. It included a worldwide, perfect temperature; unlimited food supply of fruits and grains; and a water canopy above the sky to filter out the sun's ultraviolet rays, thus preventing skin cancer. No viruses or germs were present, no mold, and no disease of any kind. My guess is that the perfect physical specimens of Adam and Eve also had a perfect metabolism and perfect food absorption ability, thus eliminating the need for urination or defecation. Why do I think this? Adam and Eve were perfect and innocent, according to Scripture. They were basically like a baby in a grown-up body. Would you put your defenseless child in an environment where they might get hurt, sick, or scared? I wouldn't. And God didn't. He said his creation was good in every way possible. Original earth was like a playpen for your own child, a perfect and perfectly safe environment in every possible way. And just as you would put your own happy baby in a playpen and leave them to enjoy the things you provided, God did the same thing. He left them alone to enjoy his gifts, but he came to be with them often to enjoy their progress and discovery. But as we all know, original earth came to an end because of the curse invoked by God after sin. This led to the second earth.

The second earth was the sin-cursed earth. God left the most beautiful angel he ever created—Lucifer, who became Satan—in charge of his children in the garden. But Satan didn't just watch them, he seduced them. How would you feel if a trusted babysitter abused your children while you were away? The sad result of all this was that Lucifer was cast out of his exalted position because of his pride, Adam and Eve were expelled from the garden of God (Eden), and they were barred access to the tree of life. But that's not all. Just as God's covenant with Noah included the animals and sea creatures (every living thing), God's curse included these same creatures. Death and disease didn't just affect humans, birds, animals, fish—all other living creatures were affected, too. If all that wasn't bad enough, things got even worse. Mankind reached the depths of depravity to such an extreme that God had to save the best from the worst (Noah and his family), send a flood to purge the evil, and start things over. Again, this affected not only the human population, but the land and all creatures worldwide.

Scientists surmise that the original water canopy—which was punctured by God and used to flood the planet—not only enabled earth to have a stable and safe environment, but it also caused the atmosphere to have a high oxygen content. One of the evidences of this is seen in the lung-to-mass ratio of many of the dinosaurs. Many of these big beasts had huge bodies, but very small lungs. They would be fine in a pre-flood environment, but would actually be unable to breathe in today's atmosphere. They would literally suffocate. This worldwide catastrophic event—the flood—led to the third earth of Scripture.

The third earth in the Bible is the post-flood earth, the one we are familiar with. Although there are many beautiful locations on our planet, they don't even compare with the original—they are a mere shadow of the former inherent beauty of a world God called good. We probably can't even imagine all the ways the original creation was superior to our world today.

But there are still two worlds left, two to come according to Scripture. Acts 3 and Romans 8 discuss the return of the King (like we see in the LORD *of the Rings*), the worldwide restoration, and the resurrection. In fact, the real crux of Christianity itself is built on restoration and resurrection. If God had eternal plans for us to simply move on and leave all this behind, he had many other appropriate words to choose from (don't forget that he invented language) and could have easily communicated that reality. But that's not the reality he plans. He plans for a merging of the current world we see and the one discussed throughout the Bible, the one we cannot see.

I don't pretend to understand it all, but somehow God plans to prove his power by fixing what Satan broke, mending what was torn apart, and blending our dimensions into his own. The One who spoke our world into existence, who keeps it spinning by his power and who hears our every prayer has fantastic plans to live with us and walk with us in daily relationship—just as he once did with Adam. And then in Isaiah 65 and 66, 2 Peter 3, and Revelation 21 and 22 , new earth will be the final frontier for us all. Huge in size, void of oceans, and a capital city almost seventeen hundred square miles are just a glimpse of what's to come. Wow. I can hardly wait, can't you?

Where or What Is Heaven?

Heaven is difficult to define. Webster's Online Dictionary offers several possibilities. The first one has interesting implications. It's listed as the dome-like sky that hovers over the entire planet. Isn't that intriguing? It is to me because one theme I noticed in the list of Bible verses connected with God and heaven centers on his home in the clouds of the sky.

One of the first examples in Scripture shows up as God descends on Mt. Sinai in a thick cloud: "Then the LORD said to Moses, 'I am going to come to you in a thick cloud so the people themselves can hear me as I speak to you. Then they will always have confidence in you'" (Exodus 19:9, NLT).

Isaiah predicts a future time of restoration of the land and the people with God present night and day in the form of a cloud: "But in the future, Israel—the branch of the LORD—will be lush and beautiful, and the fruit of the land will be the pride of its people. All those whose names are written down, who have survived the destruction of Jerusalem, will be a holy people. The LORD will wash the moral filth from the women of Jerusalem. He will cleanse Jerusalem of its bloodstains by a spirit of judgment that burns like fire. Then the LORD will provide shade for Jerusalem and all who assemble there. There will be a canopy of smoke and cloud throughout the day and clouds of fire at night, covering the glorious land. It will be a shelter from daytime heat and a hiding place from storms and rain" (Isaiah 4:2-6, NLT).

Scripture repeatedly indicates that God is close, very close. Just as a footstool for the King is close to the throne, God is apparently that close to his creation. "This is what the LORD says: 'Heaven is my throne, and the earth is my footstool. Could you ever build me a temple as good as that? Could you build a dwelling place for me? My hands have made both heaven and earth, and they are mine. I, the LORD, have spoken!'" (Isaiah 66:1-2, NLT).

In the first chapter of Ezekiel, we see a vision of God in his throne room. In the twenty-eight verses that describe this scene, sky is mentioned once and cloud is mentioned four times. As the vision continues in Ezekiel 10, the first four verses of that chapter use cloud twice more.

The prophet Daniel sees a vision of the "Son of man coming with the clouds of heaven": "I watched as thrones were put in place and the Ancient One sat down to judge. His clothing was as white as snow, his hair like purest wool. He sat on a fiery throne with wheels of blazing fire, and a river of fire was pouring out, flowing from his presence. Millions of angels ministered to him; many millions stood to attend him. Then the court began its session, and the books were opened. As my vision continued that night, I saw someone like a son of man coming with the clouds of heaven. He approached the Ancient One and was led into his presence. He was given authority, honor, and sovereignty over all the nations of the world, so that people of every race and nation and language would obey him. His rule is eternal—it will never end. His kingdom will never be destroyed. I, Daniel, was troubled by all I had seen, and my visions terrified me. So I approached one of those standing beside the throne and asked him what it all meant. He explained it to me like this: 'These four huge beasts represent four kingdoms that will arise from the earth. But in the end, the holy people of the Most High will be given the kingdom, and they will rule forever and ever.'" (Daniel 7:9-10, 13-18, NLT).

And keep in mind that all these prophets who offer us these spiritual revelations are the ones God says he always reveals things to before he does anything: "For the LORD God does nothing without revealing his secret to his servants the prophets" (Amos 3:7, ESV).

God also shows up in a cloud in the New Testament. The first time we see this is at the transfiguration of Jesus: "As the men watched, Jesus' appearance was transformed so that his face shone like the sun, and his clothes became as white as light.

Suddenly, Moses and Elijah appeared and began talking with Jesus. Peter blurted out, 'LORD, it's wonderful for us to be here! If you want, I'll make three shelters as memorials—one for you, one for Moses, and one for Elijah.' But even as he spoke, a bright cloud came over them, and a voice from the cloud said, 'This is my dearly loved Son, who brings me great joy. Listen to him'" (Matthew 17:2-5, NLT).

In the first part of Matthew 24, the disciples point out the beauty of the temple. This leads Jesus to reveal that a time will come when not one stone of the temple will be left on top of another. They are quite distraught at this news and come to him privately and ask: "Tell us, when will all this happen? What sign will signal your return and the end of the world?" (Matthew 24:3, NLT).

They thought this was just one question, because they thought that if the temple was destroyed it would be the end of the world. But as we know today, those two events don't coincide. Not even close. The temple was destroyed in 70 A. D., but the end of the world will be at least nineteen hundred years later. So, in reality, these were two separate questions. The first question was, "When will this temple be destroyed?" The second question—which will happen at a much later time—was, "Will there be a sign to signal his return and the end of this present world?"

If you understand this nuance hidden in Matthew 24, everything changes. And Jesus actually answers both questions. Obviously, many events Jesus explained in the first part of the chapter happened in 70 A.D. when Rome conquered Jerusalem. But just as obviously, Jesus continues to speak—answering the second question—and covers things that coincide with other passages about the time of the end of the current earth. Things like:

- It will be a time of greater anguish than any other the world has ever seen or will ever see again (verse 21).

- The entire population of the world would be at stake unless God intervenes (verse 22). This could only be true—in my opinion—of a nuclear threat.

- False prophets will be able to do various signs and wonders to deceive people (verse 24).

- The sun and moon will go dark and all the powers in the heavenly realms will be shaken (verse 29). Sounds like Ephesians 6 and spiritual warfare.

Here is the entire chapter for you to see for yourself if the things I have said are true. Check it out, and then go read it in whatever version you use.

> As Jesus was leaving the Temple grounds, his disciples pointed out to him the various Temple buildings. But he responded, 'Do you see all these buildings? I tell you the truth, they will be completely demolished. Not one stone will be left on top of another!' Later, Jesus sat on the Mount of Olives. His disciples came to him privately and said, 'Tell us, when will all this happen? What sign will signal your return and the end of the world?' Jesus told them, 'Don't let anyone mislead you, for many will come in my name, claiming, "I am the Messiah." They will deceive many. And you will hear of wars and threats of wars, but don't panic. Yes, these things must take place, but the end won't follow immediately. Nation will go to war against nation, and kingdom against kingdom. There will be famines and earthquakes in many parts of the world. But all this is only the first of the birth pains, with more to come. Then you will be arrested, persecuted, and killed. You will be hated all over the world because you are my followers. And many will turn away from me and betray and hate each other. And many false prophets will appear and will deceive many people. Sin will be rampant everywhere, and the love of many will grow cold. But the

one who endures to the end will be saved. And the Good News about the kingdom will be preached throughout the whole world, so that all nations will hear it; and then the end will come. The day is coming when you will see what Daniel the prophet spoke about—the sacrilegious object that causes desecration standing in the Holy Place. [Reader, pay attention!] Then those in Judea must flee to the hills. A person out on the deck of a roof must not go down into the house to pack. A person out in the field must not return even to get a coat. How terrible it will be for pregnant women and for nursing mothers in those days. And pray that your flight will not be in winter or on the Sabbath. For there will be greater anguish than at any time since the world began. And it will never be so great again. In fact, unless that time of calamity is shortened, not a single person will survive. But it will be shortened for the sake of God's chosen ones. Then if anyone tells you, 'Look, here is the Messiah,' or 'There he is,' don't believe it. For false messiahs and false prophets will rise up and perform great signs and wonders so as to deceive, if possible, even God's chosen ones. See, I have warned you about this ahead of time. So if someone tells you, 'Look, the Messiah is out in the desert,' don't bother to go and look. Or, 'Look, he is hiding here,' don't believe it! For as the lightning flashes in the east and shines to the west, so it will be when the Son of Man comes. Just as the gathering of vultures shows there is a carcass nearby, so these signs indicate that the end is near. Immediately after the anguish of those days, the sun will be darkened, the moon will give no light, the stars will fall from the sky, and the powers in the heavens will be shaken. And then at last, the sign that the Son of Man is coming will appear in the heavens, and there will be deep mourning among all the peoples of the earth. And they will see the Son of Man coming on the clouds of heaven with power and great glory. And he will send out his angels with the mighty blast of a trumpet, and they will gather his chosen ones from all over the world—from the farthest ends of the earth and heaven. Now learn a lesson from the fig tree. When its branches bud and its leaves begin to sprout, you know that summer is near. In the same way, when you see all these things, you can know his return is very near, right at the door. I tell you the truth, this generation will not pass from the scene until all these things take place. Heaven and earth will disappear, but my words will never disappear. However, no one knows the day or hour when these things will happen, not even the angels in heaven or the Son himself. Only the Father knows. When the Son of Man returns, it will be like it was in Noah's day. In those days before the flood, the people were enjoying banquets and parties and weddings right up to the time Noah entered his boat. People didn't realize what was going to happen until the flood came and swept them all away. That is the way it will be when the Son of Man comes. Two men will be working together in the field; one will be taken, the other left. Two women will be grinding flour at the mill; one will be taken, the other left. So you, too, must keep watch! For you don't know what day your LORD is coming. Understand this: If a homeowner knew exactly when a burglar was coming, he would keep watch and not permit his house to be broken into. You also must be ready all the time, for the Son of Man will come when least expected. A faithful, sensible servant is one to whom the master can give the responsibility of managing his other household servants and feeding them. If the master returns and finds that the servant has done a good job, there will be a reward. I tell you the truth, the master will put that servant in charge of all he owns. But what if the servant is evil and thinks, 'My master won't be back for a while,' and he begins beating the other servants, partying, and getting drunk? The master will return unannounced and unexpected, and he will cut the servant to pieces and assign him a place with the hypocrites. In that place there will be weeping and gnashing of teeth.'

Matthew 24 (NLT)

Note also in verse 30 that at the second coming, Jesus arrives on the clouds.

The Strongest Indicator of the God-Cloud Connection

Psalm 104 indicates specifically that God lives in the clouds: "Praise the LORD, I tell myself; O LORD my God, how great you are! You are robed with honor and with majesty; you are dressed in a robe of light. You stretch out the starry curtain of the heavens; you lay out the rafters of your home in the rain clouds. You make the clouds your chariots; you ride upon the wings of the wind. The winds are your messengers; flames of fire are your servants" (Psalm 104:1-4, NLT).

And these passages in Psalm are indications of the synonymous nature of heaven, sky, and clouds:

Sing to the one who rides across the ancient heavens, his mighty voice thundering from the sky. Tell everyone about God's power. His majesty shines down on Israel; his strength is mighty in the heavens.

Psalm 68:33-34 (NLT)

He opened the heavens and came down; dark storm clouds were beneath his feet. Mounted on a mighty angel, he flew, soaring on the wings of the wind. He shrouded himself in darkness, veiling his approach with dense rain clouds. The brilliance of his presence broke through the clouds, raining down hail and burning coals. The LORD thundered from heaven; the Most High gave a mighty shout. He shot his arrows and scattered his enemies; his lightning flashed, and they were greatly confused. Then at your command, O LORD, at the blast of your breath, the bottom of the sea could be seen, and the foundations of the earth were laid bare.

Psalm 18:9-15 (NLT)

The heavens proclaim the glory of God. The skies display his craftsmanship.

Psalm 19:1 (NLT)

Learning a Lesson from the Fig Tree

One more important aspect of the words of Jesus in Matthew 24 was his reference to the fig tree, centered on verse 32:

And then at last, the sign that the Son of Man is coming will appear in the heavens, and there will be deep mourning among all the peoples of the earth. And they will see the Son of Man coming on the clouds of heaven with power and great glory. And he will send out his angels with the mighty blast of a trumpet, and they will gather his chosen ones from all over the world—from the farthest ends of the earth and heaven. "Now learn a lesson from the fig tree. When its branches bud and its leaves begin to sprout, you know that summer is near. In the same way, when you see all these things, you can know his return is very near, right at the door. I tell you the truth, this generation will not pass from the scene until all these things take place."

Matthew 24:30-34 (NLT)

The fig tree was used in the Old Testament as a symbol for Israel. In the middle of this list of signs of the end he throws in this reference to the fig tree, connecting the fig tree blossoms to the generation of people who will be alive at the second coming. I've always been intrigued by this connection. A few years ago, I visited a Messianic Jewish church in San Diego, California. Messianic Jews are Jews who hold on to their Jewish heritage, usually participate in Jewish holidays, but also accept Jesus of Nazareth as the Messiah predicted by the Old Testament prophets. The main difference I noticed from other Christian churches I have attended was that they called the New Testament the "new covenant." Messiah was to bring a new covenant, and that's just what Jesus did.

Upon arrival at this particular congregation, each guest received a free book, *The Fig Tree Blossoms,* written by Paul Liberman. The book went into great detail to point out that the fig tree was a symbolic name for the Jewish people and that the sign of the fig tree blossoming was a reality of this current generation.

Here's how it was laid out: the blossoming of the fig tree is a symbolic representation of a large portion of end times Jews recognizing the fact that Jesus of Nazareth is actually the long-awaited and anticipated Messiah. This is significant in the face of the fact that the Orthodox Jew doesn't recognize Jesus as the Messiah. The Orthodox Jew actually uses the truths about the first coming of Jesus to prove he is not the Messiah. Let me explain how the thought process goes.

The Christian says, "The Old Testament prophecies prove that Jesus is the Messiah. Notice that Isaiah 6:9-10 says that the Messiah will speak and teach in parables. That's exactly what he did. And this passage is even quoted in Matthew 13:14-15 in the New Testament—new covenant if you prefer—and emphasizes this point!"

To this the Orthodox Jew replies, "Have you considered going back to the prophet Isaiah and reading the rest of the chapter? Verse 3 says the whole earth will be filled with his glory. At present, I would ask you to observe that the whole earth is corrupt. Verse 4 says he will be in the temple. I ask you to notice that the temple is temporarily destroyed. Isaiah 9 reveals that the government will rest on his shoulders. Jesus of Nazareth was never in charge of the government. It also says that everyone will convert their swords into plows, wars and fighting will cease permanently, and peace will prevail throughout the planet. Jesus of Nazareth didn't bring peace. He caused war. Remember the Crusades? Ever heard of the atrocities that Christians have committed throughout the ages? Selling indulgences and buying their way to heaven for a dead relative has been offered by the agents of Christian churches through the centuries. No, my friend, Jesus doesn't fulfill the predictions of Messiah. A few rumored healings and a missing body from a tomb don't prove anything. When Messiah comes, the whole world will know!"

What do you say to that? How can you convince people to take a few supposed predictions from Old Testament scripture, point to Jesus, and say, "See, he fulfilled these—literally, and that proves his identity as Messiah" when Jews point to the same Scriptures and say, "You can't pull out some selected parts as literal and claim symbolism for the rest. Who would decide which ones were literal?"

The day before Christ's ministry began, when none of the prophecies were fulfilled, they all seemed unlikely. What's the answer? I would offer this possibility for all ethnic groups to consider: There are over one hundred prophecies about the first coming that were fulfilled literally, and we use those to prove Jesus as Messiah, LORD, and King. There are over three hundred prophecies about the second coming—revealing the ultimate importance of that future event—that have yet to be fulfilled. It they are all literal—and this appears likely—then Jew and Christian are both right.

We still can point to the first coming and show how the literal fulfillment of these—one hundred percent—offers a mode of operation that God will literally fulfill the second coming prophecies—one hundred percent literal. When and if you accept this possibility, the entire Bible needs revisiting. Read it in light of this possibility, and you'll be shocked at how it makes all the complicated and integrated predictions fit and make sense, thus making Christian and Jew both correct in their assessments.

Jesus was called "Wonderful Counselor, Mighty God, and Prince of Peace," and the government will rest on his shoulders one day (Isaiah 9). Permanently.

The Merging of Heaven and Earth

"I heard every creature in heaven and on earth and under the earth and in the sea. They sang: 'Blessing and honor and glory and power belong to the one sitting on the throne and to the Lamb forever and ever.'" (Revelation 5:13, NLT).

This teaches that God will one day be praised by all living creatures—including animals and sea life—forever. Satan wants us to believe that he has permanently spoiled God's favorite planet, but God knew all along what would happen and rested in the foreknowledge of his resurrection and restoration plans. This verse also teaches that earth's animals and sea creatures will be around forever praising the King. Forever? Yes. That's what it says.

What conclusion can we surmise from this passage? The dimensions of earth and heaven will be merged permanently some day into the eternal, perfect kingdom of God.

Premise: Heaven Is Wherever God Is

If heaven is wherever God is, then the original creation—the perfect earth—was part of heaven. God walked with Adam in the garden; they talked daily and had fellowship and relationship. Then everything came apart—literally. Sin caused the borders of heaven to be temporarily redrawn, so to speak. The sin-cursed earth had to be expelled from the realm God regularly came in contact with because God—in his essence—cannot come in direct contact with anything sin-stained. When he does appear on earth throughout Scripture, notice that purification fires always insulate him from the ugliness here.

Jesus came to change all that. Jesus came to reclaim what Satan stole through deception. He came to bring the seventh and final covenant—the new covenant—between God and Christians. He came to pave the pathway to resurrection and restoration. In short, he came to fix what was broken: the people and the planet. God's covenant with Noah included the animals and sea life (Genesis 9:8-11), and Jesus's work in building us a bridge back to God included offering himself up for our sins and opening the door to the restoration of the planet itself (Romans 8:19-23).

So if heaven is wherever God is, if God walked freely on earth in the perfect garden, if earth was "expelled" temporarily from the domain of heaven because of sin, and if God plans to remove sin and death when Jesus returns, then this passage appears to be the remerging of these two dimensions. There is currently a curse on the planet (Genesis 8:21). But Revelation 22:3-5 promises that God will remove that curse before he makes his home here with us. "No longer will there be a curse upon anything. For the throne of God and of the Lamb will be there, and his servants will worship him. And they will see his face, and his name will be written on their foreheads. And there will be no night there—no need for lamps or sun—for the Lord God will shine on them. And they will reign forever and ever" (Revelation 5:13, NLT).

Finally, notice that this passage in Romans that discusses the promise of our new, permanent, immortal body is connected to and in the same context with the removal of the curse. "Against its will, all creation was subjected to God's curse. But with eager hope, the creation looks forward to the day when it will join God's children in glorious freedom from death and decay. For we know that all creation has been groaning as in the pains of childbirth right up to the present time. And we believers also groan, even though we have the Holy Spirit within us as a fore-taste of future glory, for we long for our bodies to be released from sin and suffering. We, too, wait with eager hope for the day when God will give us our full rights as his adopted chil-dren, including the new bodies he has promised us" (Romans 8:20-23, NLT).

The Valley of Vision

Isaiah 22:1 discusses a valley of vision. My prayer is that all Christians everywhere pass through that valley. As we come out the other side of that valley, I pray our vision of heaven is improved so drastically that we are nothing short of ecstatically, uncontrollably excited to the point of being enthusiastic about heaven and our eternity with God. If we can reach this point, heaven will be in our heart and on our lips so completely that we will ooze with passion for it. Our lives will overflow with the thrill of it so completely that we will all be walking evange-lists in our daily life. That "pearl of great price"—heaven—will finally be worth everything to us.

New Earth

There are three Bible passages about new earth, but they all say basically the same thing: it replaces current earth, is much better, and is eternal. Let's look at all three passages, noting the unique things about new earth that are revealed.

Look! I am creating new heavens and a new earth, and no one will even think about the old ones anymore. Be glad; rejoice forever in my creation! And look! I will create Jerusalem as a place of happiness. Her people will be a source of joy. I will rejoice over Jerusalem and delight in my people. And the sound of weeping and crying will be heard in it no more. "No longer will babies die when only a few days old. No longer will adults die before they have lived a full life. No longer will people be considered old at one hundred! Only the cursed will die that young! In those days people will live in the houses they build and eat the fruit of their own vineyards. Unlike the past, invaders will not take their houses and confiscate their vineyards. For my people will live as long as trees, and my chosen ones will have time to enjoy their hard-won gains. They will not work in vain, and their children will not be doomed to misfortune. For they are people blessed by the Lord, and their children, too, will be blessed. I will answer them before they even call to me. While they are still talking about their needs, I will go ahead and answer their prayers! The wolf and the lamb will feed together. The lion will eat hay like a cow. But the snakes will eat dust. In those days no one will be hurt or destroyed on my holy mountain. I, the Lord, have spoken!" This is what the Lord says: "Heaven is my throne, and the earth is my footstool."

Isaiah 65:17-66:1 (NLT)

- New earth will be such a fantastic improvement that we won't even think about the old ones anymore (verse 17). Note here that "ones" is plural. The Greek word used here, *ovar*, means "ancestor (that were) before." "Were" is also a plural usage. "Ancestor that was" would be a singular reference: a single past earth. Since the plural is implied, it lends even more credence to the previous earths in the Bible that have already been discussed. Many versions read simply "former," but this doesn't negate the possibility of more than one former earth.

- New earth will include Jerusalem, which will be a place of complete happiness (verse 18).

- New earth will eventually have no more crying (verse 19) as the painful memories from our past life become a distant memory.

- New earth will include a long (possibly endless) lifespan. When you've been there one hundred years, you're just starting out (verse 20).

- New earth won't be affected by death and the passage of time; no one will be in a hurry because time is short. You can take your time and build something or plant something with the full knowledge you will be around to finish it, enjoy it, or harvest it (verse 21).

- New earth's residents won't be threatened with the possibility of invasion or overthrow of the people or government (verse 22).

- New earth will have animals, but the meat-eating animals will return to a pre-flood situation when animals ate only grass and grain—not each other. Therefore, lions and lambs will cohabitate in serenity and safety (verse 25).

- New earth will include God's presence—his feet will be firmly planted on terra firma (verse 1 of chapter 66).

- "We are looking forward to the new heavens and new earth he has promised, a world filled with God's righteousness" (2 Peter 3:13, NLT).

- New earth will be filled with God's righteousness—good people with all good thoughts. This would automatically eliminate all ungodly people and evil activities. The good and meek will actually inherit new earth, as Jesus said in the Sermon on the Mount.

Then I saw a new heaven and a new earth, for the old heaven and the old earth had disappeared. And the sea was also gone. And I saw the holy city, the new Jerusalem, coming down from God out of heaven like a bride beautifully dressed for her husband. I heard a loud shout from the throne, saying, "Look, God's home is now among his people! He will live with them, and they will be his people. God himself will be with them. He will wipe every tear from their eyes, and there will be no more death or sorrow or crying or pain. All these things are gone forever." And the one sitting on the throne said, "Look, I am making everything new!" And then he said to me, "Write this down, for what I tell you is trustworthy and true." And he also said, "It is finished! I am the Alpha and the Omega—the Beginning and the End. To all who are thirsty I will give freely from the springs of the water of life. All who are victorious will inherit all these blessings, and I will be their God, and they will be my children. But cowards, unbelievers, the corrupt, murderers, the immoral, those who practice witchcraft, idol worshipers, and all liars—their fate is in the fiery lake of burning sulfur. This is the second death." Then one of the seven angels who held the seven bowls containing the seven last plagues came and said to me, "Come with me! I will show you the bride, the wife of the Lamb." So he took me in the Spirit to a great, high mountain, and he showed me the holy city, Jerusalem, descending out of heaven from God. It shone with the glory of God and sparkled like a precious stone—like jasper as clear as crystal. The city wall was broad and high, with twelve gates guarded by twelve angels. And the names of the twelve tribes of Israel were written on the gates. There were three gates on each side—east, north, south, and west. The wall of the city had twelve foundation stones, and on them were written the names of the twelve apostles of the Lamb. The angel who talked to me held in his hand a gold measuring stick to measure the city, its gates, and its wall. When he measured it, he found it was a square, as wide as it was long. In fact, its length and width and height were each 1,400 miles. Then he measured the walls and found them to be 216 feet thick (according to the human standard used by the angel). The wall was made of jasper, and the city was pure gold, as clear as glass. The wall of the city was built on foundation stones inlaid with twelve precious stones: the first was jasper, the second sapphire, the third agate, the fourth emerald, the fifth onyx, the sixth carnelian, the seventh chrysolite, the eighth beryl, the ninth topaz, the tenth chrysoprase, the eleventh jacinth, the twelfth amethyst. The twelve gates were made of pearls—each gate from a single pearl! And the main street was pure gold, as clear as glass. I saw no temple in the city, for the Lord God Almighty and the Lamb are its temple. And the city has no need of sun or moon, for the glory of God illuminates the city, and the Lamb is its light. The nations will walk in its light, and the kings of the world will enter the city in all their glory. Its gates will never be closed at the end of day because there is no night there. And all the nations will bring their glory and honor into the city. Nothing evil will be allowed to enter, nor anyone who practices shameful idolatry and dishonesty—but only those whose names are written in the Lamb's Book of Life. Then the angel showed me a river with the water of life, clear as crystal, flowing from the throne of God and of the Lamb. It flowed down the center of the main street. On each side of the river grew a tree of life, bearing twelve crops of fruit, with a fresh crop each month. The leaves were used for medicine to heal the nations. No longer will there be a curse upon anything. For the throne of God and of the Lamb will be there, and his servants will worship him. And they will see his face, and his name will be written on their foreheads. And there will be no night there—no need for lamps or sun—for the LORD God will shine on them. And they will reign forever and ever. Then the angel said to me, 'Everything you have heard and seen is trustworthy and true. The LORD God, who inspires his prophets, has sent his angel to tell his servants what will happen soon."

Revelation 21:1-22:6 (NLT)

- New earth replaces the old one (verse 1).

- Now earth has no sea. There may be lakes, streams, and rivers, but no extremely large bodies of water like a sea or ocean (verse 1).

- New earth will have a capital city: New Jerusalem. It will descend from the sky (verse 2).

- New earth will have God actually living among his people—the saved or godly (verse 3).

- New earth—our eternal existence—will be characterized by crying at times, but the LORD will wipe those tears away. Note that there have to be tears in order for them to be wiped away. Then all crying will end along with death, pain, or any kind of sadness at all—forever (verse 4).

- New earth will be completely new (verse 5).

- New earth will have a fountain of youth. It will be called living water, the spring of life, fountain of life, or water of life (verse 6).

- New earth will only have people who have used the power of God to defeat evil in their life (verse 7).

- New Jerusalem on new earth will have a high, broad wall

around it with twelve entrance gates, each guarded by angels. Each gate will be named after a tribe of Israel (verse 12).

- The twelve gates are equally spread, with three on each of the four walls surrounding the city (verse 13).

- The city wall will contain twelve primary foundational stones, each engraved with the name of one of the twelve apostles (verse 14).

- The city will be enormous in size. It will probably be cube-shaped, with a square base of 1,400 miles. (It will be square at the base, and rise to a 1,400-mile-high point in the sky, like a cube or a pyramid.) This is approximately the distance from the border between North Dakota and Canada to Eagle Pass, Texas, and from New York, New York to Canadian, Texas, but it is also 1,400 miles high. The distance from the surface of the earth to the edge of our atmosphere is only about 500 miles, so this gives you some indication of the huge difference in the overall size of new earth as compared to our current earth. And remember, this is just the capital city (verse 16).

- The city wall will be 216 feet thick. And note that a standard human measurement is specified in these measurements. This seems to indicate that the dimensions revealed here are meant to excite and overwhelm us (verse 17).

- The city will be constructed out of jasper and gold (verse 18).

- God and Jesus live in the city (verse 22).

- God and Jesus's presence will actually provide the light for the city (verse 23).

- Kings and rulers from all over the world will walk into the gates (verse 24).

- The gates will never close, and there will never be night there. Since the Father and the Son are the light source, this seems to indicate that they never leave (verse 25).

- All nations will visit the city to honor the King (verse 26).

- Only the saved, only the obedient in the current world will inhabit this wonderful place (verse 27).

- The river of life will be there, flowing from under the throne of God (chapter 22, verse 1).

- The tree of life will be growing on both sides of the river of life. The leaves of this tree will heal. Also, there will be twelve months in succession—just like current earth—and a different fruit comes from these trees each month (verse 2).

- The curse on the land, put there by God when sin occurred in the garden of Eden—will be forever gone.

- God's throne and his Son, Jesus, will be there; worship will then be done in their very presence (verse 3).

- Just as in ancient times when a servant was branded with his master's unique mark, we will bear God's mark on our own foreheads (verse 4).

- Darkness will never occur, and we will reign with him there forever (verse 5).

- God inspired the prophets—including the prophecies from this book of Revelation—and specifically instructed us to pay close attention to what they said (verse 6): "The voice from the majestic glory of God said to him, 'This is my dearly loved Son, who brings me great joy.' We ourselves heard that voice from heaven when we were with him on the holy mountain. Because of that experience, we have even greater confidence in the message proclaimed by the prophets. You must pay close attention to what they wrote, for their words are like a lamp shining in a dark place—until the Day dawns, and Christ the Morning Star shines in your hearts" (2 Peter 1:17-20, NLT).

What Might Be: The Hall of Pictoglyphs

The angel and Jamie walked slowly up the hill toward one of the great halls. Each one was unique, designed for a specific purpose: to bring pleasure in a particular area—emotionally, or physically. Like the other large structures Jamie had seen from a distance, this one was on top of a large plateau, stately and majestic, with enormous pillars outside that lined the entire perimeter. As they slowly approached, it became clear that these were by far the biggest pillars and the biggest building—at least twice as large as the others—he had visited so far. Jamie realized that it would take at least ten people his size with outstretched arms to be able to reach all the way around a pillar, and he didn't even try to count them. Each building seemed to be about the width of a football field on the front side. As they walked up the incline toward the building, they approached at an angle, and it became evident that it was at least ten times as long as it was wide. Large trees—like giant redwoods—guarded it like sentinels and prevented him from seeing how far back the monument actually went.

They were completely silent as they made their final approach; the only sound Jamie heard was their own soft footfalls on the immaculate lawn as they ascended the inclined yard that led to the steps of the structure. The lawn was lined on both sides with flowers of every color, size, and shape. Their aroma alone was enough to reveal this as heaven, but the colors were richer and fuller than anything he had ever imagined. It was as if the moment would be spoiled if anyone spoke. They walked together, Jamie a half step ahead, anticipation growing stronger with each step that brought them closer to the huge, wide granite doors.

They stopped. Jamie slowly raised his head to determine the height, which had to be at least a hundred feet. The angel fixed his gaze on Jamie, reveling in the moment, sharing the excitement with his charge, anxious to explain, but patient to wait for the right moment.

"Wow. I didn't know anything this big could exist anywhere in all of creation. What is this place?"

"You might think of it as your personal walk down memory lane. It's one of the great halls with your name on it. You will visit some of the others later."

"This one is dedicated just to me? And there are others?"

"Oh, yes, Jamie, many others. This is just the first of many. I am honored to take an image-bearer for the first visit to one of his personal great halls. This one is called The Jamie Voigt Hemphill Great Hall of Pictoglyphs. Please follow me."

They traveled the last few steps up the marble steps and to the entrance, past the huge pillars silently guarding the front like gentle giants smiling at the surrounding countryside. The structure smelled like a new home, freshly scented with the clean smells of roses and honeysuckle. Inside appeared to be marble, just like the beautiful walls and surrounding columns outside. A cool breeze seemed to come from out of the dimly lit hallway ahead, and the path down the center was wide enough for at least fifty people to walk shoulder to shoulder.

After they had traversed about fifty feet, the guide stopped and turned to face his charge with a broad smile of excited anticipation, as if he were the one who was about to be the beneficiary of the waiting surprises. Suddenly—as when you turned on a light switch in a pitch-black room—the surface in front of them rippled and disappeared, and this first section came alive with color and light. It was a picture—a photograph of Jamie and his family. They were outdoors on a bright, sunny day, a gentle breeze wafting the intoxicating smells of nature all around them. They were all smiling and dressed up as if going to a special banquet or celebration. Behind them—making it a picture-perfect setting—was an ancient log cabin, complete with a smoking fireplace offering the smell of something savory, cooking slowly. It was peaceful and comforting just to gaze at it, as if somehow this scene was made just to be preserved—and enjoyed—by the family.

Mary, Jamie's wife, was sitting on a wooden stool, back straight, smile wide, and confident joy evident in the curves of the smile on her face. Her light pink shirt perfectly complemented the pastel, floor-length skirt with pink roses. A rose was in her lap, cradled gently by her left hand.

Jamie stood just behind her with his right hand resting on her right shoulder. He was dressed in a white shirt, dark blue suit, and a sporty red tie, looking dapper and friendly. His wide smile indicated the utter joy he felt in his heart, like there wasn't a care in the world because the family was together. His bright eyes and sparkling teeth weren't at all discouraged by his thinning hair. It was as if he was exactly who he should be, a perfect fit to fill the needs of the many others in his life who looked up to him, respected his wise counsel on all things godly, and honored him as friend and colleague. It was like a snapshot of perfection: perfect love from above, harmony at home, and companionship cherished—all rolled into one picture.

The bookends, their two sons, Kendal on the left and Steve on the right, were also dressed up for the occasion, smiling and content, though perhaps completely clueless of just how blessed they really were. When wisdom lives in the room across the hallway, appreciation doesn't rule the day. Taking wisdom for granted becomes the norm, and appreciation may not well up in the human heart until wisdom personified—Dad—makes his exit.

As he gazed at the scene, Jamie smiled. The memories of family and the love that flooded their home came rushing in like a tsunami. Picnics, camping trips, hunting excursions, long drives, family get-togethers, and a host of other thoughts flashed through his head like a cherished photo album, clean and neatly organized. The joys of this hall were going to exceed anything yet experienced.

Jamie studied the picture, and the angel studied Jamie, eyes wide with joy and wonder.

"Jamie, every picture you ever took—or that was ever taken of you—is in this building. And as you have probably already noticed, each one is now much more than just a snapshot. Sweet aromas, gentle breezes, and a variety of other enhancements are included with each unique picture. Not only will each one jog your memory of the event, you will remember details and experience feelings that connect you even more deeply with each one.

"I know you must be enjoying this particular picture—the King knew it was one of your favorites—but if you will just turn toward the opposite wall, you'll see the spiritually enhanced version. This will bring the wonders of your past life in the shadow lands of the post-flood earth into even clearer view. Just across from each picture is a version of the same picture that includes your guardians—the angels assigned to those who will receive salvation."

With eyes wide, and with the silence of an obedient sheep, Jamie turned one hundred-eighty degrees to face the opposite wall just as it began to illuminate with the enhanced version of the same scene. His mouth dropped open, but words didn't come.

The picture now added the unseen world to the physical reality. Enormous, muscular, stone-faced giants stood silently behind each member of the family—as if they were a permanent, unseen member. They weren't smiling as each family member was. Their faces were those of battle-weary, victory-focused warriors with a single-mindedness for care and protection that was unstoppable. Swords hung at their sides—tiny words like etched artwork adorning each one with the uniqueness of a painting by Michelangelo. They reflected light like polished diamonds, but this didn't negate their fierce design to defend the faithful.

Each warrior had one hand on his sword, ready to draw and defend in an instant. Then Jaime noticed more of their kind in the background, almost blending into the surrounding, but facing the other way—like a battle-trained fighting unit, these were guarding the perimeter. No one—man or beast, seen or unseen—would be catching this angelic host by surprise. It was obvious that their constant, unwavering vigilance was ingrained into their personality, like soldiers stationed on the border of an enemy nation.

All male, all muscular, these hulk-like towers of strength and power were messengers of the King, sent to guard these children of the kingdom until they left the temporary cocoon and burst into the real world, the realm of the King—filled with joys and pleasures unspeakable. And it was obvious that they were focused on the task of defending and protecting this Hemphill family.

Jamie stood there—soaking in each and every detail that this first pictoglyph revealed. Finally, he heard his guide say, "Jamie, would you like to step inside the pictoglyph now and examine the details more closely?"

Wonders never cease.

Chapter 7: God Promotes a Reward System

"If any of you wants to serve me, then follow me. Then you'll be where I am, ready to serve at a moment's notice. The Father will honor and reward anyone who serves me"

(John 12:26, The Message).

Dad Enjoyed Today, But Focused On Eternity

I have often thought that if we could get a better picture of heaven in the eyes of our heart, it would be much easier to live a committed life for the kingdom in the here and now. Scripture says that God put a little bit of eternity in the human heart: "God has made everything beautiful for its own time. He has planted eternity in the human heart, but even so, people cannot see the whole scope of God's work from beginning to end" (Ecclesiastes 3:11, NLT).

If a little bit of eternity is somewhere in me, hidden in some forgotten crevice, covered like dusty, forgotten boxes in the attic of my mind, then I want to get it out, dust it off, clean it up, and see what it really looks like. Don't you?

When I was growing up, Dad was a counselor and purchasing agent at Mason High School, but that wasn't all he did. Dad was what some call a jack of all trades. He would sometimes say jokingly that he was a "jack of all trades, but master of none!" He did all kinds of work for other people. He would oversee the summer work crew for the school, he was a rock mason (we built several rock fireplaces for people in the community after someone saw the one we built in our own home), he would referee at sporting events, he preached on Sundays at many little churches in the central Texas area, and he was the announcer for the home football games for thirty-eight years, which included singing the national anthem solo on the microphone every week. He was an elder in the Mason Church of Christ and a gifted Bible class teacher; he coached football before getting his master's degree in counseling from North Texas State University in Denton (we still have his letter jacket that has a patch that says, "District 9A High School Champs 1957"—the year I was born), he was a hog farmer, and he was a carpenter—we worked every day beside the contractor when we built our home out in the country. The list could go on and on. I know it sounds like I'm bragging, but as they said in old western movies, "No brag, just fact." If that list isn't impressive enough, he had Bible studies with people on a regular basis on Tuesday nights. I have no idea how many people he baptized into Christ, but people still come up to me and say, "Your dad baptized me!" He was truly an amazing man.

We worked beside Dad on a variety of different projects during our childhood. They included things like fence-building, barn-raising, concrete work, rock-laying, raising farm animals, and carpentry. Here's the kind of man Dad was: maybe we had just mixed up a wheelbarrow full of concrete to use in a rock-laying project, and someone showed up at our place for a stand-up conference with Dad. We might just dump out the concrete in a ditch, because other people's needs came first with him. Losing a few bucks from wasted concrete was nothing compared to the needs of God's most precious creation, people. Dad cared about others.

As far as projects the Hemphill boys did, one of the biggies was our hog farm. Talk about work—and stink. We had twenty-seven sows, or mama hogs. In case you hadn't thought about it, that translates into lots of pigs. Lots of pigs meant lots of stinky work. I especially remember Dad's favorite joke, because it had to do with hogs. It went something like this:

One year, there was a drought. This is a highly technical central-Texas term meaning a lack of necessary rainfall. The drought meant that there wasn't much grass for the hogs to gorge on, so everyone's hogs got skinny—a potentially unhealthy condition for hogs. But all the hog farmers noticed that Jim's hogs were still as fat as they should be. So they asked him why his hogs weren't skinny like everyone else's. He said, "Well, you remember that one little rain we got early in the season? That rain came just in time to give the oak trees enough moisture to produce a great crop of acorns. And as you know, hogs love acorns, so I go out there every day and hold up each hog so they can eat those acorns right off the tree."

One of the other hog farmers said, "You mean you go out there every day and hold every hog up to the limbs of that tree and let 'em eat those acorns?"

"Yep," says Jim.

"Don't that take a lot of time?"

"Sure," said Jim, "But what's time to a hog?"

Ecclesiastes says there is a time for everything. I think it's time to think about heaven. And in case you haven't noticed, that passage about there being a time for everything is right before the one that says God planted a little bit of eternity in the human heart. Take a look: "There is a time for everything, a season for every activity under heaven. A time to be born and a time to die. A time to plant and a time to harvest. A time to kill and a time to heal. A time to tear down and a time to rebuild. A time to cry and a time to laugh. A time to grieve and a time to dance. A time to scatter stones and a time to gather stones. A time to embrace and a time to turn away. A time to search and a time to lose. A time to keep and a time to throw away. A time to tear and a time to mend. A time to be quiet and a time to speak up. A time to love and a time to hate. A time for war and a time for peace. What do people really get for all their hard work? I have thought about this in connection with the various kinds of work God has given people to do. God has made everything beautiful for its own time. He has planted eternity in the human heart, but even so, people cannot see the whole scope of God's work from beginning to end" (Ecclesiastes 3:1-11, NLT).

Did you ever notice that several of these things listed are connected with the word reward? Words and phrases like harvest, gather stones, search, and keep. They all have to do with personal gain as a direct result of your own, unique effort. Have you ever noticed that our life in this world is structured on the reward system? We are rewarded for our work with a paycheck. We are rewarded for our efforts in school with a diploma. We are promoted to a better, higher-paying job as a reward for doing good work on a lesser job. The list goes on and on.

As a Christian, I used to think that striving for a reward from God was selfish. And selfishness is wrong, isn't it? Therefore, working hard for eternal rewards must be wrong too, right? No.

Where did I go wrong? Is it wrong to want rewards from God? Haven't you ever heard "The ground is level at the foot of the cross"? I have. And I think it programmed me to think that striving for heavenly reward must be wrong. I had the idea that heaven was completely equal for everyone and socialistic in nature.

But is it? Forrest Gump says, "That's all I got to say about that." But I want to see what God says about it. Probably two of the best authors on the subject of heaven are C. S. Lewis and Randy Alcorn. In Randy Alcorn's book, *The Treasure Principle*, he reminds us that:

> Heaven will be a place of rest and relief from the burdens of sin and suffering; but it will also be a place of great learning, activity, artistic expression, exploration, discovery, camaraderie, and service.

Some of us will reign with Christ (Revelation 20:6). Faithful servants will be put "in charge of many things" (Matthew 25:21, 23). Christ will grant some followers leadership over cities in proportion to their service on earth (Luke 19:12-19). Scripture refers to five different crowns, suggesting leadership positions. We'll even command angels (1 Corinthians 6:3).

We are given these eternal rewards for doing good works (Ephesians 6:8; Romans 2:6, 10), persevering under persecution (Luke 6:22-23), showing compassion to the needy (Luke 14:13-14), and treating our enemies kindly (Luke 6:35).

God also grants us rewards for generous giving: "Go, sell your possessions and give to the poor, and you will have treasure in heaven" (Matthew 19:21).

Jesus is keeping track of our smallest acts of kindness: "If anyone gives even a cup of cold water to one of these little ones because he is my disciple, I tell you the truth, he will certainly not lose his reward" (Matthew 10:42).

God is keeping a record of all we do for Him, including our giving: "A scroll of remembrance was written in his presence concerning those who feared the LORD and honored his name" (Malachi 3:16).

Imagine a scribe in heaven recording each of your gifts on that scroll. The bike you gave to the neighbor kid, the books to prisoners, the monthly checks to the church, missionaries. All are being chronicled. Scrolls are made to be read. I look forward to hearing your giving stories and meeting those touched by what you gave.

By clinging to what isn't ours, we forego the opportunity to be granted ownership in heaven. But by generously distributing God's property on earth, we will become property owners in heaven!

Wow. Now that's the place I want to be. Heaven will be a place of rest and relief from burdens, a place without suffering, and a place to learn new things. Learning will be for sheer enjoyment rather than just because it will be on the next test.

Our hog farm—stink as it did—accomplished one very good thing in my life: it paid for my first year of college at Abilene Christian University. Mom didn't work until I got older, and Dad taught school, so we didn't have much money. ACU was quite expensive, especially for a small-town boy on a small-town budget, where a date often consisted of getting a cherry vanilla Coke at the Dairy Queen with two straws. I wasn't sure how I could afford college. That's where the hogs came in handy.

Dad taught us early about managing money. I think I started my own checking account in the seventh grade. It wasn't uncommon for me to have several dollars in a jar in my room from various lawn-mowing jobs or post-hole digging projects for ranchers in the area. Dad wanted me to learn the value of money: how hard it is to accumulate and how easy it is for it to disappear. I would ride my bike—an old thing we rescued from the dump grounds and spray-painted silver—to the bank three blocks away and fill out my own deposit slip. Then I rode back up the hill to our house and entered the receipt in my thin-lined journal where I had been instructed to carefully record each check I wrote in one column and each deposit I made in another. The far right-hand column was reserved for something very special: the balance.

Each month when my own, personal, individual, big-person bank statement came—I loved seeing the personalized address on the front with my name on it instead of Dad's—I was required to reconcile my records with those of the Mason National Bank to make sure I didn't get overdrawn, a condition not readily understood by many today. As I saw this account slowly build from the initial five-dollar deposit on the first day to huge sums of fifteen, twenty-five, and eventually fifty dollars, I began to feel rich. Rich is a relative term meant to separate you from other kids your age whom you assumed to be without the privilege of their own, personal, individual, wonderful checking account with their own name appearing in the window of those colorful green envelopes marked "bank statement" each month.

I later discovered that rich was a short-lived term. In Dad's patient teaching style, I began to learn the second part of this most valuable life lesson: how quickly that same money could disappear. The Western Store was only two doors down from Underwood's Food Store on the corner of the downtown square, and I had to ride my bike right past The Western Store to show up for my part-time job at Underwood's. Bonnie and Amos Underwood lived right across the street from our home on Live Oak, and they provided gainful employment on occasion to young boys needing part-time work. I was one of those young boys and proud of it, since jobs for teens were quite hard to come by—especially in small towns. At a dollar and seventy-five cents per hour, which took quite a while to work up to, I saw my bank account swell to above the fifty dollar mark, so I was ripe for the pickin', so to speak. With the knowledge of my large balance in my personal account tucked securely in my pea-sized brain—I had just reconciled my bank statement—I rode by those big display windows at The Western Store and stopped short. I had never seen such a thing of beauty. In that window was a new display containing one of the most beautiful pair of cowboy boots I had ever seen. They were sleek and black, but somehow when the light hit them, they had almost a green, almost glittery look. I know that sounds ugly now, but trust me, at the time they were beautiful. Strikingly so. And they really looked special with the green leisure suit on the manikin above. It was checkered hounds-tooth slacks with a solid green jacket to match. I had never seen a leisure suit at the time, and just like everyone else, I was destined to grow to hate them later, but at that time it was the latest thing and quite cool. And I wanted it. Bad.

I must have talked about it to Bonnie, because I remember she took me there a few days later and bought me that suit as a gift. I was never prouder. I wore it to church that very next Sunday and received many "oohs" and "aahs" and "Where did you get that?" comments. I had to explain over and over that it was called a leisure suit and that it was the latest thing.

My bank account, however, wasn't near as tickled because it had been completely depleted. At the base of those beautiful slacks, supporting the entire color-coordinated outfit, were those black-green boots. I had paid for the boots with my own money. Dad made me pay so I could learn that second lesson—money disappears fast. I would learn the next month when the next personalized bank statement arrived that they charge you a service charge when you let your account dip below five dollars, so I had to do a few more odd jobs for neighbors to build that account back up to the required five-dollar minimum. Boy was that depressing. But I sure was enjoying my new clothes.

That was my junior year. The summer after my senior year at Mason High School, I was preparing for my new life's adventure in Abilene, Texas. I was excited. But it dawned on me that I was in trouble as I realized how expensive college would be. I had always known that I would have to pay for it myself, but armed with the knowledge that just one pair of boots can deplete a checking account rather quickly, I wasn't sure how we could make this college thing happen.

Thus enters the solution for the freshman year: the Hemphill Hog Farm. Dad called a meeting, and all three board members were in attendance: me, Dad, and my brother Kendal. Dad's solution to my financial dilemma was to sell my part of the hog farm (one third) and send the money to ACU. Problem solved.

I can't remember a problem he couldn't fix. Just like my heavenly Father. I think that God's purpose for fathers in the world is to be a fragrance of him in each family. Satan, however, realizes this, so his main objective is to destroy the relationship between fathers and their children. He knows that if we don't trust our earthly father we will have a very difficult time trusting our heavenly Father. I believe this is the primary reason that Satan is so busy attacking families today. If the father relationship is damaged or nonexistent in the earthly realm, then it will be even more difficult to have a healthy relationship with our unseen Father.

I remember lots of great family Bible studies when I was growing up. We often had a short Bible study at home. We went to Bible class at the church three times a week, and there were gospel meetings quite often. These usually involved a special out-of-town speaker. These meetings were on a variety of subjects and usually very interesting, but I don't remember a single sermon or study on heaven.

Paul said it like this:

> Remember that in a race everyone runs, but only one person gets the prize. You also must run in such a way that you will win. All athletes practice strict self-control. They do it to win a prize that will fade away, but we do it for an eternal prize. So I run straight to the goal with purpose in every step. I am not like a boxer who misses his punches. I discipline my body like an athlete, training it to do what it should. Otherwise, I fear that after preaching to others I myself might be disqualified.
>
> (1 Corinthians 9:24-27, NLT)

I've thought about that a lot more as I've gotten older and seen more and more relatives die. Heaven is our goal, yet we don't ever talk about it until someone we know goes there.

How do athletes maintain the clarity of focus and discipline needed to train properly and reach their goal? They focus and concentrate on the goal. Why don't we do that as Christians?

I don't know, but I hope that changes. So let's talk about the heavenly rewards God promises.

God Promotes a Reward Economy

Scripture points out repeatedly that God promotes a reward economy. Passage after passage bears this out. Let's look at just a few.

"Afterward the Lord spoke to Abram in a vision and said to him, 'Do not be afraid, Abram, for I will protect you, and your reward will be great'" (Genesis 15:1, NLT).

David was rewarded for killing Goliath: "David received the same reply as before: 'What you have been hearing is true. That is the reward for killing the giant'" (1 Samuel 17:27, NLT).

God rewards people for doing good deeds and for being loyal to him: "'Here is your spear, O king,' David replied. 'Let one of your young men come over and get it. The Lord gives his own reward for doing good and for being loyal, and I refused to kill you even when the Lord placed you in my power, for you are the Lord's anointed one'" (1 Samuel 26:22-23, NLT).

Those who trust in their own riches also have a reward: "Let them no longer trust in empty riches. They are only fooling themselves, for emptiness will be their only reward" (Job 15:31, NLT).

Rewards from God last forever:

Day by day the Lord takes care of the innocent, and they will receive a reward that lasts forever.

Psalm 37:18 (NLT)

Judgment will come again for the righteous, and those who are upright will have a reward.

Psalm 94:15 (NLT)

Evil people get rich for the moment, but the reward of the godly will last.

Proverbs 11:18 (NLT)

God's rewards aren't reserved only for the future. Some rewards are for our present enjoyment:

Live happily with the woman you love through all the meaningless days of life that God has given you in this world. The wife God gives you is your reward for all your earthly toil.

Ecclesiastes 9:9 (NLT)

A man can do nothing better than to eat and drink and find satisfaction in his work. This too, I see, is from the hand of God, for without him, who can eat or find enjoyment?

Ecclesiastes 2:24-25 (NIV)

We must trust God, for other rewards are reserved for the future:

But all will be well for those who are godly. Tell them, 'You will receive a wonderful reward!'

Isaiah 3:10 (NLT)

Yes, the Sovereign LORD is coming in all his glorious power. He will rule with awesome strength. See, he brings his reward with him as he comes.

Isaiah 40:10 (NLT)

I replied, 'But my work all seems so useless! I have spent my strength for nothing and to no purpose at all. Yet I leave it all in the LORD's hand; I will trust God for my reward.'

Isaiah 49:4 (NLT)

For I, the LORD, love justice. I hate robbery and wrong-doing. I will faithfully reward my people for their suffering and make an everlasting covenant with them.

Isaiah 61:8 (NLT)

The LORD has sent this message to every land: 'Tell the people of Israel, Look, your Savior is coming. See, he brings his reward with him as he comes.'

Isaiah 62:11 (NLT)

I always thought that rewards in heaven were equally distributed; that somehow, God was a socialist. Ephesians 2:9 teaches salvation is not a reward for our good works, it is a free gift that is distributed equally to all who are obedient, but God plans to reward you based on the deeds you have done. I even found a verse that says in heaven, the amount of clothing we will wear is directly proportional to the number of good deeds we have done. Revelation 19:7-8 says, "Let us be glad and rejoice and honor him. For the time has come for the wedding feast of the Lamb, and his bride has prepared herself. She is permitted to wear the finest white linen' [Fine linen represents the good deeds done by the people of God.]" (NLT).

Reward, then, is based on your current activities for the kingdom. Since our deeds are all completely different, just as each part of the body of Christ is different, our rewards then must also be different. Notice what Jeremiah says about it: "You have all wisdom and do great and mighty miracles. You are very aware of the conduct of all people, and you reward them according to their deeds" (Jeremiah 32:19, NLT).

God also offers special rewards for those who have faced any kind of persecution, whether it be worldly persecution or persecution within the church itself: "God blesses you when you are mocked and persecuted and lied about because you are my followers. Be happy about it! Be very glad! For a great reward awaits you in heaven. And remember, the ancient prophets were persecuted, too" (Matthew 5:11-12, NLT). Those ancient prophets weren't persecuted by the Gentiles; they were persecuted by their own people. Does that still happen today? You bet it does.

It's interesting to notice here in Matthew that Jesus teaches you can actually lose your eternal reward if you do the good to be admired by others or for any other reason than getting a reward directly from him:

Take care! Don't do your good deeds publicly, to be admired, because then you will lose the reward from your Father in heaven. When you give a gift to someone in need, don't shout about it as the hypocrites do— blowing trumpets in the synagogues and streets to call attention to their acts of charity! I assure you, they have received all the reward they will ever get. But when you give to someone, don't tell your left hand what your right hand is doing. Give your gifts in secret, and your Father, who knows all secrets, will reward you. And now about prayer. When you pray, don't be like the hypocrites who love to pray publicly on street corners and in the synagogues where everyone can see them. I assure you, that is all the reward they will ever get. But when you pray, go away by yourself, shut the door behind you, and pray to your Father secretly. Then your Father, who knows all secrets, will reward you. (Matthew 6:1-6, NLT).

And when you fast, don't make it obvious, as the hypocrites do, who try to look pale and disheveled so people will admire them for their fasting. I assure you, that is the only reward they will ever get. But when you fast, comb your hair and wash your face. Then no one will suspect you are fasting, except your Father, who knows what you do in secret. And your Father, who knows all secrets, will reward you. Matthew 6:16-18 (NLT)

There are no secrets with God, including your motivation for the deeds you do. You can fool others, but you can't fool him. If you do the right thing for the wrong reason, it may benefit others, but it won't benefit you. Lots of verses indicate levels of reward:

"If you welcome a prophet as one who speaks for God, you will receive the same reward a prophet gets. And if you welcome good and godly people because of their godliness, you will be given a reward like theirs" (Matthew 10:41, NLT).

"If the master returns and finds that the servant has done a good job, there will be a reward" (Matthew 24:46, NLT). And believe me, the Master is returning some day, perhaps someday soon.

God says there will be great reward for any who have experienced mocking or hatred because they acknowledge Jesus Christ as the Son of God: "God blesses you who are hated and excluded and mocked and cursed because you are identified with me, the Son of Man. When that happens, rejoice! Yes, leap for joy! For a great reward awaits you in heaven. And remember, the ancient prophets were also treated that way by your ancestors" (Luke 6:22-23, NLT).

More and more, I began to notice that God's rewards are specific. They are appropriate to the deed. Again, every deed is different; therefore, it follows that every reward is different:

Love your enemies! Do good to them! Lend to them! And don't be concerned that they might not repay. Then your reward from heaven will be very great, and you will truly be acting as children of the Most High, for he is kind to the unthankful and to those who are wicked.

Luke 6:35 (NLT)

Then at the resurrection of the godly, God will reward you for inviting those who could not repay you.

Luke 14:14 (NLT)

I tell you, use your worldly resources to benefit others and make friends. In this way, your generosity stores up a reward for you in heaven.

Luke 16:9 (NLT)

Dad always taught me to use my resources wisely. I just never realized that my heavenly Father linked my rewards to the wise use of those resources: "When he returned, the king called in the servants to whom he had given the money. He wanted to find out what they had done with the money and what their profits were. The first servant reported a tremendous gain—ten times as much as the original amount! 'Well done!' the king exclaimed. 'You are a trustworthy servant. You have been faithful with the little I entrusted to you, so you will be governor of ten cities as your reward.' The next servant also reported a good gain—five times the original amount. 'Well done!' the king said. 'You can be governor over five cities' " (Luke 19:15-19, NLT).

Once I started noticing this biblical principle of reward being in direct proportion to my deeds, I saw it everywhere. It is repeated over and over. These two guys were both faithful with what they had been given. They both doubled the investment they were entrusted with through wise management of the resources they were given. And their rewards were proportionate to their faithfulness. But it was not equal. The rewards were appropriate to their capabilities, but different for each.

Losing rewards you could have had will be a sad reality: "But there is going to come a time of testing at the judgment day to see what kind of work each builder has done. Everyone's work will be put through the fire to see whether or not it keeps its value. If the work survives the fire, that builder will receive a reward. But if the work is burned up, the builder will suffer great loss. The builders themselves will be saved, but like someone escaping through a wall of flames" (1 Corinthians 3:13-15, NLT).

Here we have a graphic illustration of the salvation of the individual, but a loss of rewards. This also reinforces the idea that salvation is a gift but rewards are earned. Good deeds must pass through the fires of judgment to be of additional benefit to the person who makes it into the kingdom.

"Salvation is not a reward for the good things we have done, so none of us can boast about it" (Ephesians 2:9, NLT).

"Remember that the LORD will reward each one of us for the good we do, whether we are slaves or free" (Ephesians 6:8, NLT). Do we all accomplish the exact same amount of good? No. The implication here is that the reward is proportionate to our good deeds.

"Dear brothers and sisters, I love you and long to see you, for you are my joy and the reward for my work. So please stay true to the LORD, my dear friends" (Philippians 4:1, NLT).

Part of Paul's reward is the knowledge that he had a part in the salvation of these people. But don't forget, Paul's influence is still being felt today because of his writings and the writings about him. The resulting additions to God's kingdom will also be added to his reward. Our lives are like that, too. Our influence for the kingdom can be felt long after we die by the way the lives of our friends and relatives are changed as a direct result of our influence.

Dad died at the relatively young age of sixty-nine. But several people came to Christ as a direct result of his death. They came to the funeral. The place was packed and people stood around the wall, filling even the foyer to pay their respects. Some drove an hour to attend the funeral, only to find cars lining the streets up to two blocks away. Being near his lifeless body, no doubt, made his words to them ring like bells in their heads. "God loves you and wants you to be in heaven with him some day! Won't you please choose Christ?" Then they couldn't resist. Several were soon baptized and joined the kingdom.

Others came back to the LORD as a direct result of Dad's death. They had left the fellowship of other Christians and returned to a worldly life. They came to the funeral too, and Dad's words must have vibrated in their heads as well: "We miss you; we love you; won't you come back into fellowship?" They did. I know they did because they told me or my brother or our mother.

We cried. We cried for our loss, but we also cried for joy because the kingdom of God would be bigger as a direct result of the influence of the man we called "Dad." Our loss was the kingdom's gain, in more ways than one. That doesn't mean it hurts less. If anything, it made me feel the loss even more, but we knew somehow it was for the best. It was for God. It was within the will of God. He knows the best time for everything. There's a time to die. Are you ready?

One close family friend called Mom, crying loudly on the telephone. He had worked with Dad, had asked him for advice, and he truly loved Dad for his kind, giving heart. "Oh, Mary, why did God have to take Jamie? Why couldn't he have taken me instead? He was such a good man!" At the time, this individual was living a lifestyle in submission to alcohol.

I will never forget Mom's response. "Jamie was ready. You need to get ready! God loves you and wants you to go to heaven some day, too." Mom hung up the phone and we both cried.

I cry for you too, reader. Dad was ready. Are you ready? You'd better get ready. The death rate is currently at one hundred percent. Death is unavoidable, unless Jesus comes in your lifetime. Either way, time is short. I pray this prayer for you:

> LORD, *I pray for everyone who reads this. I pray that you will create circumstances in their lives that cause them to choose you before it's too late. I pray their hearts will change;*

I pray that they will be obedient to your word all the way through to baptism. I pray their lives will change and that their influence will cause many more to enter the kingdom. In Jesus's name, Amen.

Many of us have had the wrong idea about a reward system. I think it's rooted in our American culture. We are used to a system where my winning of a prize knocks someone else out of a prize. Not so with God's reward economy. There are no limits to his treasures. Just because one person gains an enormous amount of treasure as a direct result of working for the kingdom, there are no fewer treasures available for others. God's treasure chest is bottomless. And remember, it's his idea in the first place: Matthew 6:19-20 says, "Do not store up for yourselves treasures on earth, where moth and rust destroy, and where thieves break in and steal. But store up for yourselves treasures in heaven, where moth and rust do not destroy, and where thieves do not break in and steal" (NIV).

We know that selfishness is wrong; therefore, we have believed that to store up treasure for ourselves must also be wrong. Not according to God. He just says, "Stop storing up treasures here and start storing up treasures there." Notice that Paul yearns for others to receive their rewards:

"I don't say this because I want a gift from you. What I want is for you to receive a well-earned reward because of your kindness" (Philippians 4:17, NLT).

"Physical exercise has some value, but spiritual exercise is much more important, for it promises a reward in both this life and the next" (1 Timothy 4:8, NLT).

This passage adds another dimension. It reminds me of a statement I once heard from Rick Warren, who wrote *The Purpose-driven Life*: "Every day you draw closer to God is a successful day. Every day you do not draw closer to God—I don't care if you made a million dollars—is an unsuccessful day."

I believe in physical exercise. I have to. I'm a diabetic. I have been on insulin for over thirty years. I think that puts me on borrowed time, but then, aren't we all on borrowed time—God's time? I believe what Dr. David Jeremiah once said: "God's man doing God's will is immortal until God is ready to take him." If I don't exercise, my blood sugars run higher, and I don't feel good. But how many of us believe, really believe, in the daily discipline of spiritual exercise?

I like to get up early. That's when I spend time in prayer and in God's word. It saddens me to hear retired people talk at the McDonalds where I go each day. Their lives sound so futile, so self-centered. How different their lives and their conversation would be if they focused on kingdom things–eternally different.

> Do not throw away this confident trust in the LORD, no matter what happens. Remember the great reward it brings you!
>
> Hebrews 10:35 (NLT)

> It was by faith that Moses, when he grew up, refused to be treated as the son of Pharaoh's daughter. He chose to share the oppression of God's people instead of enjoying the fleeting pleasures of sin. He thought it was better to suffer for the sake of the Messiah than to own the treasures of Egypt, for he was looking ahead to the great reward that God would give him.
>
> Hebrews 11:24-26 (NLT)

> And remember that the heavenly Father to whom you pray has no favorites when he judges. He will judge or reward you according to what you do. So you must live in reverent fear of him during your time as foreigners here on earth.
>
> 1 Peter 1:17 (NLT)

But even if you suffer for doing what is right, God will reward you for it. So don't be afraid and don't worry.

1 Peter 3:14 (NLT)

And when the head Shepherd comes, your reward will be a never-ending share in his glory and honor.

1 Peter 5:4 (NLT)

Watch out, so that you do not lose the prize for which we have been working so hard. Be diligent so that you will receive your full reward.

2 John 8 (NLT)

These Scriptures also seem to indicate that it's possible to receive less than your full reward. How? By doing fewer good deeds for the kingdom than you were created to do. I use this prayer often:

LORD, *help me to accomplish all you created me to accomplish— not one thing less, because that would be wasteful, and not one thing more, because that would be prideful. In Jesus' name, Amen.*

Finally, note this seventh from the last verse in the Bible. John just can't end this book of prophecy without one more admonishment about rewards that Jesus will bring when he returns:

"See, I am coming soon, and my reward is with me, to repay all according to their deeds" (Revelation 22:12, NLT).

After I noticed all these verses about God's rewards, my perspective changed about heaven.

What Might Be: A Place in the Capital City

They had shifted again—they arrived in another large room, but this one was beautifully decorated with paintings, pictures, lovely furniture, and every comfort and convenience imaginable. Jamie was overwhelmed at the sight.

"It's beautiful! Who lives here?"

"This may surprise you, Jamie, but this place is yours."

"Mine? You've got to be kidding. I don't deserve this!"

"No one does. But that doesn't stop the King from being generous to his faithful children. Let me show you around and let you meet a few of your servants."

"I have a servant too?"

"Of course. You have many servants, but you will only meet a few of them today—we have much to see and do. There's a party for you in the central complex this afternoon, and I just want to show you a small portion of this place right now."

The angel touched the wall to his left, and the surface shimmered briefly, then became transparent—right before their eyes. The view was nothing short of spectacular. That's the only word that Jamie could think of to describe it—there really wasn't an adequate word, at least not in his language. You could see for thousands of miles. Light was everywhere. There were mountain ranges; rocky crags; soft, flowing valleys; streams and rivers everywhere; and beautiful gazebos sprinkled around all the lakes in the distance, as far as he could see. Everything appeared manicured, like a team of white-robed gardeners had removed every dead leaf or limb, trimmed every tree like a park, and mowed and manicured around every bush and shrub. Even the smells from the panoramic scene wafted right through the transparent wall, giving the experience an unexpected dimension.

Then Jamie noticed that all the land sloped gently away from where they were, as if this was the highest place in the world. The creeks, streams, and rivers all flowed away, downhill from them. He could see canoes, barges, yachts, and boats of every kind—all moving back and forth on the rivers and lakes.

"It's unbelievable."

"Believe it, Jamie. It's real, it's permanent, and this is your personal apartment—forever."

"Apartment? How can you simply call it an apartment? It's huge."

"This isn't your only eternal dwelling. You might think of it as your place in the city, a room in your Father's house. Remember, he promised you a room."

"Oh, yes, I remember. I loved the songs we sang about heaven and being with God. One of them called our future home a 'mansion.' I would say this certainly qualifies."

At this, the angel laughed out loud. He even bent over slightly, as if this was so funny he could hardly contain himself. It was the first real burst of emotion Jamie had seen from him yet.

"What's so funny?" Jamie felt like he'd just missed the punch line of an excellent joke.

"Forgive me, Jamie, but this isn't your mansion. Rest assured, you have one, but this isn't it."

"What do you mean?"

"As I already told you, consider this your apartment in the capital city. We will visit your mansion another day.

"We are on floor seven thousand in New Jerusalem, the capital city of the eternal King. When you put on Christ in baptism because of your faith in Jesus as God's Son, he adopted you into the family—he entered into a permanent covenant relationship with Jamie Voigt Hemphill. You changed your name. You called yourself Christian from that day forward. The pact was sealed, the future assured. That day, the Carpenter began working on your place here in the Father's house. He promised you there was room for you, and there is. The furniture, the layout, the decorations, and all the amenities were designed specifically for you to enjoy.

"Please, walk through and take a quick look around. You have forever to enjoy it, but we have a full schedule today, so take a short look and we'll move on."

Jamie was awestruck. The room they were in now was bigger than a baseball field back home. Gold was everywhere. Diamonds, rubies, and a variety of other precious stones adorned various objects around the room. Seven large fireplaces were scattered around the room, beautiful couches and uniquely shaped chairs formed a semi-circle around each one—perfect for groups of friends to enjoy coffee, snacks, and intimate discussion.

At the far end of the room, he noticed a door. It took a few minutes to get there, but he suddenly had the urge to see where it went, to know what was behind it. He turned the gold knob easily with his hand—no moans or squeaks like the doors on earth—it opened fluidly, as if on perfect hydraulic hinges, and swung back out of the way.

It took his breath away. The treasures were abundant, unique, without description, and scattered throughout the room. He looked back at his guide in disbelief.

"It's all yours, Jamie. Pick out one gift and touch it."

"Touch it?"

"Yes, touch it. Each gift is unique. The Carpenter has not only constructed this structure especially for you, he also fashioned special surprises into each piece. Pick one and lay your hand on it."

Jamie looked around the room and immediately noticed a familiar object. It was a decorative, colorful bluebonnet, a Texas wildflower. He walked toward it. The special smell and vivid colors reminded him of his home in the Texas Hill Country near Brady, Texas. It began to gently sway—as if a breeze suddenly entered the room. With each step that brought him closer to the flower, Jamie noticed other new senses he now possessed—indescribable in the English language—that took this simple experience to new heights. It was much bigger than the ones he remembered back home, but everything was bigger here, wasn't it? He slowly reached to touch the soft, blue petals. The moment contact was made, his head exploded in a cacophony of memories and experiences. Suddenly, he visualized every scene in his life—even those he was far too young to remember—that involved bluebonnets.

He saw himself sitting in a cradle with his siblings around him as his mother, Irene, took a photo with a square, boxy camera. He saw himself with his own 35mm camera doing the same thing with his own two boys many years later. He saw himself at about the age of sixty-five with all six of his grandsons posing and smiling as his son Steve took a shot with a new, fancy digital unit. Scene after scene flashed by. He felt himself smiling at the memories, overwhelmed at the wonderful emotions, content to stand right there forever and just enjoy this one, simple flower.

Oh, the joys of living with the King, of having a room in his house. Forever. The thought then crossed his mind about how much he would enjoy gathering his loved ones to this *little* apartment in the capital city for food, fun, and family. And to think, this was just a short, quick stop this morning because they had much more to see and do today. Awesome. A tear of joy trickled down his cheek, and then he felt an unseen hand gently wipe it away.

"Thank you, Lord. I love you, Lord."

It was all he could think to say at the moment.

Chapter 8: Reunion

"I miss you a lot, especially when I remember that last tearful good-bye, and I look forward to a joy-packed reunion"

(2 Timothy 1:4, The Message).

My Brother Kendal's Memories of Dad

Although I never thought I would become a writer, I'm proud to say that my brother Kendal is a writer. Literally. He writes weekly articles for a group of central Texas newspapers and monthly articles for hunting and fishing magazines. One of the outdoor magazines that carries a monthly article written by him is *Texas Fish & Game*. A couple of years after Dad died, Kendal shared a personal story that revealed Dad's generous, loving heart. It truly gives you a glimpse of the man we grew up loving. I think you'd get a better snapshot of Dad and a better understanding of our excitement about our future reunion with him if you read the account in Kendal's words:

> The cold winter sky seemed to press down on us, threatening snow, stiffening our fingers and invading our lungs with every breath. We had been walking for a couple of hours, and night was not far off. We were headed back toward the pickup, with little chance of making it before we ran out of daylight. Even so, every time I whispered and pointed to a log, Dad stopped and we sat and rested for a few minutes.
>
> I was probably seven or eight, excited to be on my first

real hunt with my father instead of just riding around in the pickup with the heater running, looking for deer out the window.

I remember thinking how neat it was to be able to get Dad to stop whenever I wanted him to. We would whisper for a while, Dad still hoping for a shot, and then he would ask if I was ready, and we would get up and walk some more.

Like most Texas kids, I learned about hunting and fishing from my father, begging to go every time he left the house. Having a brother almost four years older who got to go a lot sooner than I did made things seem terribly unfair. Still, Dad took me whenever he could, and I cannot remember a time when he went hunting or fishing without one or both of us tagging along.

I was 10 the first time I got to go hunting alone, and Dad gave me some loaded-down shells he had found for his .243. He showed me where to sit the day before the season opened, and pointed out where I would see a deer.

I huddled under my bush the next morning, shivering with cold, barely able to stay awake after a night rendered sleepless by excitement. When I could finally see, I looked where Dad had pointed and, sure enough, in a few minutes a doe stepped out and gave me an easy, broadside shot.

If my dad had told me the sun was going to come up in the west, I would have bet the farm on it.

He met me halfway to the house, almost as excited as I was, and helped me field dress my deer and take it to the barn. When I asked him why he wasn't hunting, he pointed to the rifle I was holding and said, "That's the only gun I've got." I felt three inches high. I couldn't believe Dad had passed up hunting on the first day of the season just so I could go alone.

Dad sacrificed for his family all his life.

Now that Dad is gone, I find myself wondering who's going to pick me up when I stumble, dust off the seat of my pants, and get me going again. I realize how much I depended on him, and how much I took him for granted…give your children something money cannot buy: your time. A father's most important job is being a dad to his kids. Anyone can be a father, but it takes a special guy to be a dad…

That hunt with Dad? The sky was dark long before we got out of the woods that day, and snowflakes were falling by the time we got back to the pickup. I wasn't worried. I knew we would get back okay, and I was snug and warm, anyway. Dad had taken off his coat and put me on his back, and then put his coat back on over me.

He couldn't button it in front, but at least one of us was warm and dry. Seems like that kind of thing happened a lot over the years.

Instant Gratification: Today's Mantra

The world today is focused on instant gratification, drive-through convenience, and no waiting—for anything. The world wants what it wants, and it wants it now, and it's trying its best to teach us all to be that same way. But the King has a different plan: work hard for him just a little while—seventy or eighty years of life—and then enjoy an unbelievably great forever. But most have said "no" to this offer. We prefer to trade in a $10 billion inheritance —that's $10,000,000,000—for a $100 per week allowance. Are you making that mistake? Are you willing to change that habit? I pray we all do.

Thanks for allowing me to give you a peek into my Dad's life. I hope his style and my observations about it will inspire you to take on the deferred gratification outlook on life, and—more importantly—work to take others with us into a fantastic eternity. Literally.

> LORD, *help me change the world. Bless my work, and may it help the world to get excited about heaven and eternity. Forgive us for having traded in an incalculable inheritance for a small, immediately spendable pittance right now and help me to be willing to trade that allowance back in to you for an eternity of wealth. In Jesus's name, Amen.*

Commanded to Think About Heaven

> Since you have been raised to new life with Christ, set your sights on the realities of heaven, where Christ sits in the place of honor at God's right hand. Think about the things of heaven, not the things of earth. For you died to this life, and your real life is hidden with Christ in God.

> Colossians 3:1-3 (NLT)

Note: The Greek word here used for "set your sights" is "zeteo," and means a philosophical search or quest; just like "seek the lost" from Luke 19:10 is present tense, indicating a command to do this on an ongoing basis. It means to diligently, actively pursue with single-mindedness.

Heaven-Centered Thinking

What is heaven-centered thinking? It's going through the Bible teachings about heaven and then contemplating them, meditating on them, and considering them. Further, it's having those verses and thoughts in the back of your mind as you read other passages of Scripture.

Now, what does heaven-centered thinking cause? Well, I can't speak for everyone, but I can tell you what it's caused in my life. It's caused peace. As I read passages describing the last days as perilous times, my new opinion of heaven gives me peace in the middle of all my daily struggles.

It's caused confidence. As I began to realize God's pattern of prophetic fulfillment throughout the Bible was a literal fulfillment, I began to grow confident that God's promises about eternity are just as real and literal. When I discovered that all the first-coming passages of Jesus came true literally, I suddenly felt sure God would do everything he promised for me, too. Literally.

It's caused faith. My faith in God and in his eternal plan grew and grew, and I began to read the Bible with a renewed joy in a purpose-driven faith.

It's caused excitement. I now have a great anticipation and excitement for what God has planned for our eternal future.

It's caused evangelism. When I really got excited about heaven, I suddenly realized that I wanted to take as many people with me as I possibly could.

It caused prayer. Prayer is a great—but often unused—method of evangelism. If we pray for circumstances to occur in the lives of others that cause them to realize their need for a Savior, there's nothing they can do—they are completely defenseless against our prayers.

Heavenly Citizenship

Scripture teaches that this current world is not our home. Our home is coming here later, possibly meaning after the restoration: "For this world is not our permanent home; we are looking forward to a home yet to come" (Hebrews 13:14, NLT).

How would the meaning have been changed if it had said, "We look forward to being taken to the city"? That would have given this statement a completely different meaning, wouldn't it?

Our permanent citizenship is promised to begin after our bodily transformation, after Jesus returns. "But we are citizens of heaven, where the LORD Jesus Christ lives. And we are eagerly waiting for him to return as our Savior. He will take these weak mortal bodies of ours and change them into glorious bodies like his own, using the same mighty power that he will use to conquer everything, everywhere" (Philippians 3:19-21, NLT).

Kingdom Secrets

Some say, "Don't waste your time studying about heaven" because 1 Corinthians 2:9 says, "No eye has seen, no ear has heard, and no mind has imagined what God has prepared for those who love him" (NLT).

But notice that the context of the passage suggests a very different thought. "When I am among mature believers, I do speak with words of wisdom, but not the kind of wisdom that belongs to this world or to the rulers of this world, who are soon forgotten. No, the wisdom we speak of is the mystery of God— his plan that was previously hidden, even though he made it for our ultimate glory before the world began. But the rulers of this world have not understood it; if they had, they would not have crucified our glorious LORD. That is what the Scriptures mean when they say, 'No eye has seen, no ear has heard, and no mind has imagined what God has prepared for those who love him.'

But it was to us that God revealed these things by his Spirit. For his Spirit searches out everything and shows us God's deep secrets. No one can know a person's thoughts except that person's own spirit, and no one can know God's thoughts except God's own Spirit. And we have received God's Spirit (not the world's spirit), so we can know the wonderful things God has freely given us. When we tell you these things, we do not use words that come from human wisdom. Instead, we speak words given to us by the Spirit, using the Spirit's words to explain spiritual truths. But people who aren't spiritual can't receive these truths from God's Spirit. It all sounds foolish to them and they can't understand it, for only those who are spiritual can understand what the Spirit means. Those who are spiritual can evaluate all things, but they themselves cannot be evaluated by others. For, 'Who can know the Lord's thoughts? Who knows enough to teach him?' But we understand these things, for we have the mind of Christ" (1 Corinthians 2:6-16, NLT).

Paul saw heaven, and with that background, notice his prayer: "I pray that your hearts will be flooded with light so that you can understand the wonderful future he has promised to those he called. I want you to realize what a rich and glorious inheritance he has given to his people" (Ephesians 1:18, NLT).

Notice his outlook on life. "For to me, living is for Christ, and dying is even better. I am torn between two desires: Sometimes I want to live, and sometimes I long to go and be with Christ. That would be far better" (Philippians 1:21, 23, NLT).

Christ is also the head of the church, which is his body. He is the beginning, supreme over all who rise from the dead. So he is first in everything. For God in all his fullness was pleased to live in Christ, and through him God reconciled everything to himself. He made peace with everything in heaven and on earth by means of Christ's blood on the cross.

(Colossians 1:18-20, NLT)

How does Christ's sacrifice make peace with every*thing*? What's the difference between everything and everyone? It's not just the people he sacrificed for; it's the planet, too.

Plato's Heaven Versus Christian Heaven

Many Christians today have a different view of eternity than the biblical one. Plato was one of the first human desecrators of eternity. He came to the conclusion that all flesh was evil by nature; therefore, our future eternal existence with God must be only spiritual. How does this conflict with Scripture? Genesis 1:31 states that everything in the physical creation was very good, "God looked over all he had made, and he saw that it was very good!" (NLT). All creation was physical, tangible, real, but it was also good; in fact, it was very good. It was so good that God wanted to visit Adam every day in that beautiful garden.

Western culture has influenced the church to the point that many Christians fail to read their Bible on a regular basis, leaving them to be influenced by popular opinion instead of inspired Scripture. N. T. Wright mentions in his new book, *Surprised by Hope*, that Plato's view of heaven was "disembodied bliss" rather than the biblical picture of a new heaven and new earth. He goes on to say, "The biblical vision of the future world is a vision of the present cosmos renewed from top to bottom by the God who is both creator and redeemer" (80).

Parables Offering Eternal Insights

There are two parables in Matthew 13 that Jesus uses to give us a deeper and fuller understanding of the kingdom. Here's the first one:

> The kingdom of heaven is like a farmer who planted good seed in his field. But that night as the workers slept, his enemy came and planted weeds among the wheat, then slipped away. When the crop began to grow and produce grain, the weeds also grew. The farmer's

workers went to him and said, "Sir, the field where you planted that good seed is full of weeds! Where did they come from?" "An enemy has done this!" the farmer exclaimed. "Should we pull out the weeds?" they asked. "No," he replied, "you'll uproot the wheat if you do. Let both grow together until the harvest. Then I will tell the harvesters to sort out the weeds, tie them into bundles, and burn them, and to put the wheat in the barn. "

Matthew 13:24-30 (NLT)

Consider the possibility that this parable—for those who will accept it—teaches that heaven is earth with all evil and evil people removed and purified by fire. Just a few verses later, Jesus explains this illustration, confirming this possibility.

The Son of Man is the farmer who plants the good seed. The field is the world, and the good seed represents the people of the kingdom. The weeds are the people who belong to the evil one. The enemy who planted the weeds among the wheat is the devil. The harvest is the end of the world, and the harvesters are the angels. Just as the weeds are sorted out and burned in the fire, so it will be at the end of the world. The Son of Man will send his angels, and they will remove from his kingdom everything that causes sin and all who do evil. And the angels will throw them into the fiery furnace, where there will be weeping and gnashing of teeth. Then the righteous will shine like the sun in their Father's kingdom. Anyone with ears to hear should listen and understand!

Matthew 13:37-43 (NLT)

According to Jesus's own interpretation of his own parable, the field—the earth—is the kingdom. And at the end, evil and evil people will be removed from the kingdom. How much plainer could it be?

Is this difficult to accept? For some it may be. But—more importantly—is it the truth? Sure looks like it, doesn't it? Is it a salvation issue? Not really. But could it become a motivational tool to encourage lost people to become Christians and for Christians to fulfill their God-designed destiny by becoming more focused on bringing people into the kingdom before it's eternally too late? Probably. It's surely done that for me. I became much more focused on kingdom things and lost souls after I came to this realization than I was before.

Greeting the Coming King

Consider the possibility that the triumphal entry gives us a glimpse of the second coming. Notice what the people did when the news swept through the city that Jesus was on the way.

> The next day, the news that Jesus was on the way to Jerusalem swept through the city. A large crowd of Passover visitors took palm branches and went down the road to meet him. They shouted, 'Praise God! Praise God! Blessings on the one who comes in the name of the LORD! Hail to the King of Israel!'
>
> John 12:12-13 (NLT)

What did the people do when they heard the King was coming? They left the city and went out on the road to meet him there. Then they accompanied him into the city shouting, "Hosanna." Do you know what Hosanna means? It is a Hebrew word that means "Please come save us now."

Now compare this scene to the second coming, described in 1 Thessalonians.

> We tell you this directly from the LORD: We who are still living when the LORD returns will not meet him ahead of those who have died. For the LORD himself

will come down from heaven with a commanding shout, with the voice of the archangel, and with the trumpet call of God. First, the Christians who have died will rise from their graves. Then, together with them, we who are still alive and remain on the earth will be caught up in the clouds to meet the LORD in the air. Then we will be with the LORD forever. So encourage each other with these words.

1 Thessalonians 4:15-18 (NLT)

Many have assumed that since the dead and the living will rise to meet Christ in the air that we will then all go somewhere else for eternity rather than simply escorting the King back here to earth, an earth in desperate need of the restoration God promised to perform. They assume the greeting of the King in the clouds would necessitate an abandonment of the sin-sick world, but that isn't stated anywhere in Scripture. In fact, it would contradict all the other teachings, especially the second coming prophecies.

We know Scripture doesn't contradict itself, so how would this view properly fit into other passages giving great detail like this one directly from the mouth of our LORD: "The Son of Man will send his angels, and they will remove from his kingdom everything that causes sin and all who do evil. And the angels will throw them into the fiery furnace, where there will be weeping and gnashing of teeth. Then the righteous will shine like the sun in their Father's kingdom" (Matthew 13:41-43, NLT).

The only way I can think of that these very specific teachings would not contradict each other is to view the triumphal entry as a part of the second coming. Then it seems to make sense, doesn't it?

We go out to greet the coming King—in the air—and

accompany him back to the kingdom—the earth he promised to restore—shouting his praises and celebrating the moment. As he arrives, the dead Christians come back from an intermediate state of paradise to earth with him (Revelation 17:14). Then they are reunited with their body from the grave or the sea, and are transformed into immortals—just as the living are also transformed into immortals—and the King restores the planet to a worldwide Eden where he can live with us, walk with us, and have relationship with us forever. Purification fires will have cleansed the planet and removed all evil and all evil people—including the curse itself.

Good People Will Inherit the Land Forever

David, the man after God's own heart, wrote in many Psalms that the land was to be a permanent inheritance of the godly, and that the evil, ungodly people would be removed. Psalm 37 is just one example. Here are some selected verses from that chapter in the New Living Translation.

Verse 1: "Trust in the LORD and do good. Then you will live safely in the land and prosper."

Verse 9: "The wicked will be destroyed, but those who trust in the LORD will possess the land."

Verse 10: "Soon the wicked will disappear. Though you look for them, they will be gone."

Verse 11: "The lowly will possess the land and will live in peace and prosperity."

Verse 18: "Day by day the LORD takes care of the innocent, and they will receive an inheritance that lasts forever."

Verse 20: "The wicked will die. The LORD's enemies are like flowers in a field—they will disappear like smoke."

Verse 22: "Those the LORD blesses will possess the land, but those he curses will die."

Verse 27: "Turn from evil and do good, and you will live in the land forever."

Verse 29: "The godly will possess the land and will live there forever."

Verse 34: "He will honor you by giving you the land. You will see the wicked destroyed."

Verse 35-36: "I have seen wicked and ruthless people flourishing like a tree in its native soil. But when I looked again, they were gone!"

We Will Rule With Christ

Genesis 1:26-28 reveals that humans were created to rule. Paul confirms this in 2 Timothy 2:12 by saying we will rule with him in eternity. But did you know that there's a Bible verse that tells exactly where we will rule? Earth. Here's the verse:

> They sang a new song with these words: "You are worthy to take the scroll and break its seals and open it. For you were slaughtered, and your blood has ransomed people for God from every tribe and language and people and nation. And you have caused them to become a kingdom of priests for our God. And they will reign on the earth."
>
> Revelation 5:9-10 (NLT)

Work in Eternity

"On the seventh day, having finished his task, God rested from all his work" (Genesis 2:2, NLT).

God is in heaven. He rests. Will we rest in heaven? If he rests, wouldn't it be logical that we would also rest? If he does work that causes him to look forward to rest, why wouldn't we? Doesn't the idea of rest carry with it the implication that we will be active in a task of some kind? If it only meant that we will rest from our kingdom work before we die, wouldn't we get tired of resting after a few hundred years? I believe the more likely interpretation here is that we will work for the king, serving him in various ways, and then enjoy seasons of rest—just as God does.

Eating in Eternity

> In Jerusalem, the LORD Almighty will spread a wonderful feast for everyone around the world. It will be a delicious feast of good food, with clear, well-aged wine and choice beef. In that day he will remove the cloud of gloom, the shadow of death that hangs over the earth.
>
> Isaiah 25:6-7 (NLT)

Here we learn that the LORD is planning a huge banquet for everyone around the world. The physical world is round, so this is an indication that the eternal new earth will also be round. The banquet will have the best food and drink we have ever tasted. And the feast already has a scheduled date. When will it be? It will be the same day that death is removed.

"But there is an order to this resurrection: Christ was raised as the first of the harvest; then all who belong to Christ will be raised when he comes back. After that the end will come, when he will turn the kingdom over to God the Father, having destroyed every ruler and authority and power. For Christ must reign until he humbles all his enemies beneath his feet. And the last enemy to be destroyed is death. For the Scriptures say, 'God has put all things under his authority.' (Of course, when it says 'all things are under his authority,' that does not include God himself, who gave Christ his authority.) Then, when all things are under his authority, the Son will put himself under God's authority, so that God, who gave his Son authority over all things, will be utterly supreme over everything everywhere" (1 Corinthians 15:23-28, NLT).

Recognizing Others in Eternity

Jesus took Peter and the two brothers, James and John, and led them up a high mountain to be alone. As the men watched, Jesus' appearance was transformed so that his face shone like the sun, and his clothes became as white as light. Suddenly, Moses and Elijah appeared and began talking with Jesus. Peter blurted out, "LORD, it's wonderful for us to be here! If you want, I'll make three shelters as memorials—one for you, one for Moses, and one for Elijah."

Matthew 17:1-4 (NLT)

This is known as the transfiguration, but note that these disciples had never seen Moses and Elijah—they had died many years before Peter was born—but they recognized Moses and Elijah immediately. This appears to confirm that in eternity we will immediately recognize and know people we've heard about but never met.

Needing Water in Eternity

The rich man shouted, Father Abraham, have some pity! Send Lazarus over here to dip the tip of his finger in water and cool my tongue, because I am in anguish in these flames. But Abraham said to him, son, remember that during your lifetime you had everything you wanted, and Lazarus had nothing. So now he is here being comforted, and you are in anguish. Then the rich man said, "Please, Father Abraham, at least send him to my father's home. For I have five brothers, and I want him to warn them so they don't end up in this place of torment."

Luke 16:24-25, 27-28 (NLT)

There are several interesting things we can learn from these two verses. In this parable, the rich man remembered his ungodly brothers and wanted someone to go back to warn them. This indicates continuity of memory and accurate recollection of his life's previous circumstances before his death. If that quality weren't present, it wouldn't really even be you going to heaven or hell, would it? The absence memory to connect your good or bad deeds to your eternal destiny—the joy of being in heaven because of your obedience or the agony of being in hell because of your disobedience—would cause a complete disconnect between the current you and the future you. It would be almost like it would be someone else—not you—who went into a future existence.

Additionally, notice that the suffering of the flames in hell was physical, and there was the desire for water to ease that suffering. This dead man wanted water—a physical, earthly, tangible substance. This indicates he had a physical, tangible body in eternity.

Heavenly Clothing

You will wear clothing in eternity. You will be lavishly adorned based on the most unusual material. "For the time has come for the wedding feast of the Lamb, and his bride has prepared herself. She is permitted to wear the finest white linen. [Fine

linen represents the good deeds done by the people of God.]"
(Revelation 19:7-8, NLT).

Still Having Difficulty?

No wonder my heart is glad, and I rejoice. My body rests
in safety. For you will not leave my soul among the dead
or allow your holy one to rot in the grave. You will show
me the way of life, granting me the joy of your presence
and the pleasures of living with you forever.

Psalm 16:9-11 (NLT)

For those still having difficulty with this whole idea of a real,
tangible, physical, earthly eternity, consider again this passage
from Psalm 16. This passage is about King David, and it's also
about Jesus. Double prophecies are common in Scripture, but
this is one of the best examples because it's easy to connect both
events it points to. In chronological order, the first resurrection
here is referred to by the words, "your holy one," and is the resurrection of Jesus. But the yet unfulfilled second one is referred
to by the other pronouns "my," and "me" is the resurrection of
David to a physical, earthly existence that includes cohabitation
with the Lord. The King of Israel—David—will rise to cohabitate with the King of kings—Jesus—forever.

No One Can Stop God's Plan to Do All This

I am God, and there is no other; I am God, and there
is none like me. I make known the end from the beginning, from ancient times, what is still to come. I say: My
purpose will stand, and I will do all that I please. From
the east I summon a bird of prey; from a far-off land, a
man to fulfill my purpose. What I have said, that will
I bring about; what I have planned, that will I do. Lis-

ten to me, you stubborn-hearted, you who are far from righteousness. I am bringing my righteousness near, it is not far away; and my salvation will not be delayed. I will grant salvation to Zion, my splendor to Israel.

Isaiah 46:9-13 (NIV)

The Joy of Family Reunions

Do you remember getting excited about going to a family reunion when you were growing up? I do. They were fun to me. Why? There are lots of reasons.

First of all, we always seemed to have our reunion in a place that was fun to visit. I remember having several get-togethers at Richards Park in Brady, Texas. As a little kid, Richards Park was huge to me. Humongous. Colossal. When we got out of our old Chevy and gawked up at the monkey bars, swing sets, and slide that looked like they touched the sky, we thought we had died and gone to heaven.

Are we expecting heaven's reunion to be so different? You know, as I study God's Word more and more, I have begun to use this prayer:

> LORD, *I am about to read your Word. You know what you meant when you wrote it; help me to know what you mean as I read it. In Jesus's name, Amen.*

It's funny, but when I use that prayer before I study, I see things I never saw before. I also like to think about what some have called "God's telephone number," or Jeremiah 33:3, which says, "Ask me and I will tell you some remarkable secrets about what is going to happen here" (NLT).

I think he wants us to ask. I think he's anxious to tell us more. The real question is, are you really interested? Do you want to learn more? I do.

The Atheist at Burger King

Note: Real name changed to protect the guilty.

Burger King isn't exactly the place you expect to find an atheist, but they are cropping up in all kinds of unexpected places, so I guess I shouldn't have been surprised when I found one there or rather, one found me. I have discovered, sadly, that when someone sees you in this day and time reading your Bible in a public place like Burger King, they assume you are a preacher. It had happened on several occasions, but on this one particular day, it was a quite different experience—scary, to be exact.

Usually when people saw me reading the Scriptures and chose to speak to me about studying God's word, they'd say, "Where do you preach?"

I would politely say, "I'm not a preacher, I'm just a businessman."

Oftentimes, they would get a funny look on their face, like it was the strangest thing they ever saw, in a shocked sort of way they would ask, "Why are you reading the Bible?" I would respond that I was preparing to teach a Bible class or that I was working on Bible thoughts to put on my prayer web site called Prayer Thoughts (at www.prayerthoughts.com). That would be it. But this particular day was quite different. I'll never forget it.

I was sitting in a booth, my regular spot in the corner, a place by the window with plenty of light for reading. An elderly gentleman with long, white curly hair plopped down in my booth before I even saw him coming and sat right across from me. He looked a little like the pictures of the genius Albert Einstein, but without the mustache. He smiled and greeted me in a quite friendly fashion and said, "Where do you preach?"

So far, nothing unexpected, considering my track record of at least one or two people asking me the same question every week. I had developed this habit of early-morning Bible study alone and had practiced it religiously for about seven years. I offered my standard answer, "I'm not a preacher," but this didn't lead to the logical and normal line of questioning that so often had followed this mundane beginning. In fact, I don't even think he heard me answer. He started telling me about a Bible story that I was familiar with, and then he made some observations about that particular story.

I sat there, a little shocked at this unexpected turn of events, but slowly began to tune in to the points he was making about the passage. This was my second shock: he was wrong about the events in the story, and his recounting of the "facts" in the selected story had resulted in some equally incorrect deductions.

When he finally paused to take a breath, I politely opened my Bible to the passage and read the details that he had misquoted and misapplied. This led him to attempt to begin an argument, which I was not about to engage in, given the bizarre circumstances surrounding the entire event. As his lips moved, an epiphany jolted my brain, reminding me of a passage I had just been studying and welling in my mind as an unexpected opportunity to test the biblical teaching from that passage.

I had just been reading two passages that teach that if a person can't verbalize the statement "Jesus is LORD," that person has a spirit other that the Holy Spirit. In other words, they have a demon or a demon spirit:

"This is how we know if they have the Spirit of God: If a person claiming to be a prophet acknowledges that Jesus Christ came in a real body, that person has the Spirit of God" (1 John 4:2-3, NLT).

"No one speaking by the Spirit of God will curse Jesus, and no one can say Jesus is LORD, except by the Holy Spirit" (1 Corinthians 12:3, NLT).

The thought that exploded in my brain said, *Test this Bible teaching. Ask this man if Jesus is* LORD. I had never done this in my life, but I've done it many times since, and several times the answer that came was shocking. *So,* I thought, *here I go.*

Dr. Smith was a retired professor from a major secular university out in the west. "Excuse me, Dr. Smith," I said, "is Jesus LORD?" What happened next was so surprising and so rapid-fire that even now I have chills up and down my spine thinking about what he said and did.

First of all, he leaped up from our booth there at Burger King. In fact, his exit was so fast that my mind had trouble processing it, like the blurry feet of Wylie Coyote as he gears up for chasing the Road Runner. Dr. Smith was in his late sixties or early seventies, so the shock I felt from this explosion of movement was considerable.

The next thing I noticed was his demeanor. His angry look, clinched jaw, gritting teeth, hunched back, and index finger pointing right in my face all caused me to feel what I can only describe as utter shock. Then his words reached my ears, and my brain began to process the loud, audible response, "No—who is Jesus anyway?" came through those gritting teeth. "Who is God?" he continued. "I don't know who that is."

As I look back on it now, I realize how intricately the Holy Spirit of God was leading me to the right—or best—words at that exact moment. This revelation lead me to a surprising response from Dr. Smith, and the end result is that I'm much better prepared for the battle between good and evil, the great spiritual battle between Satan and God.

I looked up at his face—only inches from my own—and smiled. Then I said, "I'm going to pray for you that one day you will know Jesus as LORD."

His quick response to this new idea was a scream—right there in Burger King—as every head turned to look. "No. Don't pray for me."

Now I spoke softly right to him. I leaned in closer and smiled, saying, "I will."

He turned around and stomped through the exit and out to his car. He knew he couldn't stop me. He was completely defenseless against my prayers for him.

I never saw Dr. Smith again, but I have learned to ask the simple question, Is Jesus LORD? to many people over the years since then. It's quite revealing. It's direct. It's simple. It tells you exactly where people stand; no guessing. I encourage you to ask all your friends and acquaintances this same question. And be ready to pray for them when you get the wrong answer. Be soft. Whisper if it helps. But smile. Then pray. Heaven will be fuller because of it, and your reward will be great. See you there.

What Might Be: The Welcome Party

The stage was set. The guests had all arrived. The King stood at the back of the spacious hall, Reunion Hall. His nail-scarred hands hung loosely by his side; his damaged feet bore the scars as well. He was smiling—that contented "it's almost time" smile he used for just such occasions.

This was one of the great halls used to welcome new arrivals. It was filled with handpicked guests, all with unique ties to the new arrival: Steven Blane Hemphill, first-born son of Jamie Voight Hemphill. It was as if time stood still. No one felt rushed or anxious—those emotions don't exist here. An indescribable contentment permeated every being present, as it did the entire kingdom. Time didn't actually stand still; it moved forward. But it didn't matter because no one aged, all was calm, each person completely at ease.

They all stared at the enlarged portal as it began to glow where Steve and his escort would appear. Although quiet in nervous, excited anticipation was the order of the day, you could hear a giggle here and there as it broke the electric silence. Just as all image-bearers mark and celebrate their earthly birthday, this day would be remembered—for eternity.

The first wave of greeters was those from Steve's immediate family. Front and center were his father and mother, Jamie and Mary Hemphill. Next to them were his grandparents, William and Irene Hemphill, and William and Patty Engdahl. The center of the room at the front by the entrance was filled with relatives, but on both sides of the family, making a semi-circle of welcome for the new arrival, were close friends who had made the journey first. High school friends who moved away, the preacher's son who had lived in Mason during junior high, kindergarten friends, college buddies, and friends from the places Steve had lived over the years were all full of smiles, honored to be invited to this special occasion.

Recording devices hung from high in the corner of each room and were also scattered along the large wooden rafters—scanning the crowd, preserving the moment. The holographic log of this arrival and subsequent celebration would be preserved for the participants to enjoy and relive anytime they wished in the millenniums to come, much like we look at a photo album of a great vacation or watch a video of our children's graduation or birthday party. Memories of all special occasions and events are continually preserved and stored to be enjoyed repeatedly in the centuries to come.

The tables scattered throughout the hall were laden with food of all kinds for everyone to enjoy, but the one closest to the entrance was filled with Steve's favorite foods: sugar cookies; pie crust with butter, cinnamon, and sugar baked on top; sopapia cheesecake; and doughnuts—piles and piles of doughnuts. After sixty years of having to discipline himself to eat right every day and taking insulin to stay alive long enough to fulfill his purpose, Steve was soon to be free to eat whatever he wanted and however much he wanted. This truly would be heaven to him—every joy fulfilled, every dreamed lived out, every friendship and love enhanced to an indescribable degree.

They watched and waited. The people were ready, the food was ready, the celebration was ready, and the King was ready. Every eye was on the portal entrance where the guest of honor would soon appear. And then he did.

But that's another story for another time. How about you; will you be there?

Faith Comes By Hearing

Faith Comes By Hearing is a ministry dedicated to providing God's Word to the nations in a format and language that the two-thirds world's oral population can understand. As of this writing, they now have the Audio New Testaments in 359 languages. The New Testaments are provided to villages, neighborhoods, churches, prisons, and schools around the world on a self-contained playback unit that is charged by a solar panel or hand crank and can be heard by a large audience in a group listening session. Since half the world's population is illiterate, I believe this is the best possible way to get the Good News about Jesus out to a lost and dying world. Faith Comes By Hearing also offers free audio downloads for all of their recordings at faithcomesbyhearing.com.